Clondeglass

Clondeglass

Creating a garden paradise

Dermot O'Neill

Photography by Dermot O'Neill   Foreword by Carol Klein

Kyle Books

First published in Great Britain in 2013 by
Kyle Books, an imprint of Kyle Cathie Ltd
67–69 Whitfield Street
London W1T 4HF
general.enquiries@kylebooks.com
www.kylebooks.com

Printer line 10 9 8 7 6 5 4 3 2 1

ISBN 978 0 85783 095 1

Editor: Judith Hannam
Editorial Assistant: Tara O'Sullivan
Proofreader: Polly Boyd
Designer: Jane Humphrey
Photographer: Dermot O'Neill
Production: Lisa Pinnell

A Cataloguing in Publication record for this title is
available from the British Library.

Colour reproduction by ALTA London
Printed and bound in Slovenia by DZS Grafik d.o.o

To the memory of my grandmother,
Hanora Hall, who encouraged my interest
in gardening from an early age.

A special thank you to Carmel Duignan and Bill O'Sullivan

for their support and help in creating this book.

CONTENTS

IX   *Foreword by Carol Klein*

1   **Introduction: Reclaiming Clondeglass**

17   **Creating Beautiful Borders**

41   **Achieving Colour Throughout the Year**

42   *Spring*

80   *Summer*

110   *Autumn & Winter*

129   **Fabulous Foliage**

130   *Purple-leaved plants*

140   *Variegated plants*

148   *Golden-leaved plants*

155   **Gardening Practicalities**

156   *Soil*

164   *Protecting your Plants*

178   *Resources*

179   *Index*

182   *Acknowledgements*

Foreword by Carol Klein

The first time I met Dermot O'Neill it was clear that he was a very special person. You could feel the love coming from him, for people and for plants. That must have been more than twenty years ago at The Chelsea Flower Show when I was a very new exhibitor. Who was this lovely, warm Irishman who exuded enthusiasm, knew every plant intimately and couldn't help but talk about them to anyone who shared his passion? Since then I've had the good fortune to meet up with him on numerous occasions and I hope to do so for many years to come.

Dermot is a storyteller of the most engaging kind, he is a gardener and a plantsperson of the highest order. The book he has written, combining these talents to tell the story of his garden, is a blissful creation.

It is a privilege to know Dermot and to be invited into his garden through the pages of this book. Immediately we are engaged in its history, enveloped in its narrative. It is unputdownable. Both words and pictures carry us on and involve us in the story – we feel the disappointment when another party makes a higher bid for the garden and the exaltation when it finally becomes his. We learn the history and the geography of the place and see Dermot's plans unfold and become reality. We are there searching for fritillaries or choosing the most exquisite roses.

His writing is honest and direct. As a gardener I find these pages packed with ideas that relate to my own garden. There is practical common sense too, for Dermot respects natural laws and abides by them when making his choices and finding the places to plant his treasures. Dermot was ever the collector, always searching out the best of the best and the rarest of the rare. But in his case, rather than just enjoying the chase and ticking off the list to move on to the next trophy, having found the plants, they are honoured and nurtured, welcome guests at the garden party. Eventually they gain residential status and become part of the whole picture.

Clondeglass is no museum, no collector's cabinet; it is a living, developing entity. It epitomises the philosophy of treating gardening as a process rather than a product. You know that, for Dermot, it will be an ongoing love affair rather than the creation of a showcase.

There are so many specific ideas, so much information about particular plants and wisdom about how to grow them, so much inspiration about what to plant together. Yet these are not ideas we necessarily want to copy blindly, more there is the desire to emulate Dermot's attitude and, through sharing the making of his garden, to cherish our own. I love the book – it will always be an inspiration, a reminder of how love can triumph over adversity as well as a glorying in creating a garden and filling it with wonderful plants.

You are in for a treat.

INTRODUCTION

Reclaiming Clondeglass

Clondeglass

Introduction

Right Nepeta 'Six Hills Giant' and vivid pink *Geranium psilostemon* bordering the sandstone path that leads up to a lattice urn planted with nasturtiums.

Below The increasingly rare red squirrel is a frequent visitor to Clondeglass.

Overleaf Vivid red 'Queen of Sheba' and 'Pink Diamond' tulips planted through grass, extra deep, to encourage repeat flowering. The box hedging has yet to be trimmed into shape. In the centre is a standard Spanish laurel, *Laurus nobilis.*

If it's possible for a garden to be part of a person, then Clondeglass is a part of me. 'Why Clondeglass?', you may say. The answer is rooted in my passion and obsession for growing plants. I don't just collect plants, I get involved with their stories, where they come from, how to grow and care for them, their history and their unique characters. And, of course, their individual beauty.

Clondeglass has allowed me to express myself in many different ways. Owning this walled garden has given me a blank canvas and the freedom to explore and experiment with growing the plants I love. Clondeglass indulges all of my senses, allowing me to touch, see, smell, hear and taste. I can bite into the first season's tomato and feel it make my mouth water with its flavour. I can inhale the scent from the first rose of the summer, enjoying its delicious aroma. I can watch the setting sun from Clondeglass as it illuminates the garden on a summer afternoon, and look on in awe as the hummingbird hawk moth hovers from flower to

flower. I can look into the eye of a red squirrel, only feet from me, as it scurries away; feel the soft velvet fur on a magnolia bud; and hear the swooshing sounds of swifts before they go to roost. These are just a few of the magical experiences to be had at Clondeglass.

It's hard to find elsewhere the peace and tranquillity that I enjoy here. Clondeglass has its own unique and uplifting atmosphere. While I was restoring it, RTÉ – the Irish national television station – approached me to make a gardening series. Just as we were about to start filming, I fell ill. I thought I had a stomach ulcer and went to my GP, who immediately sent me to the Beacon Hospital for tests. These included a biopsy, which revealed that I had a fast-growing form of stomach cancer. I was immediately admitted to St. Vincent's hospital, under the care of Professor Crown. I remember it as if it were yesterday. The evening I went in, I thought I might never leave. The nursing staff were fantastic. As I sat on the edge of the bed in tears, a nurse calmly spoke to me and comforted me. The first night was probably the most difficult, but her kind words helped enormously. I was told that I would be starting chemotherapy at once. The details were explained and I remember thinking of Clondeglass. It was the one place that stood out in my mind as a beacon of hope.

Being able to think of all the things I had planted there that were going to grow, the wonderful bulbs in place and how they were going to develop and flower gave me great comfort, plus a focus that I desperately needed at that time. I was also secure in the knowledge that, while I was away, Clondeglass was being cared for by an experienced gardener, Tanguy de Toulgoët. Clondeglass had become my sanctuary, even if only in my mind. It was a place that I could escape to and meditate on the beauty of nature and the wonderful plants I was growing there.

During my period in hospital, while undergoing chemotherapy, I was told that I would need a hole drilled in my cranium. This was frightening, but I was told it was necessary to combat the cancer cells that had been detected in my spinal fluid. Another form of chemotherapy was to be administered this way. Altogether, this was possibly the darkest period of my life. I genuinely did not believe I would survive, and yet through it all Clondeglass was there, as that special place to look forward to visiting and seeing again.

Meanwhile, RTÉ had asked if they could film my journey through this dark stage. I agreed, as I felt it would be a positive thing to do – if I could help others by sharing the experience, it would be worthwhile. So Larry Masterson and a television crew set about filming my recovery. This included a visit to Clondeglass when I was feeling well enough. In time, the series was aired and broke all viewing records for its time slot. This was a very good experience to be involved with – so positive and uplifting – and the wonderful comments, letters, cards and words of encouragement I got from the general public will always stay with me.

Today, Clondeglass is part of my everyday life. The garden has developed over the years. Plants have started to mature, experiments have come and gone, and every time I visit I feel there is a strong, positive atmosphere in the place. It is a joy and a pleasure and I love being there. Of course, it's never finished and there are always jobs to be done and plans to be made. As I write, I'm planning on resurfacing all of the paths in the garden for the coming year. The two garden pavilions that you encounter when you enter the garden through the main gates are well underway and I also have plans for a Victorian-style greenhouse. I hope that this book will give you a look inside my secret gardening world where I share my constant love and passion for growing plants and flowers.

Left The dramatic foliage of the ornamental rhubarb, *Rheum palmatum* 'Atrosanguineum', contrasts with the yellow of the double daffodils.

Below The oriental poppy *Papaver orientale* 'Patty's Plum'.

Discovering Clondeglass

Below A track laid out with hardcore after the positioning of the drainage.

Right The border with timber edging and sandstone gravel in place, and the blue-and-white ceramic seats and containers in position.

Some twelve years ago, I found myself in a difficult situation. I was not working and was behind in my bank payments. I kept pushing the problem away, thinking that somehow everything would work out and be all right, but, little by little, what with the mortgage and living expenses, I found myself getting deeper and deeper into debt. One morning it hit me that it wasn't going to get better any time soon and that I'd have to do something drastic. There and then I made the decision to sell my house, pay the bank and look forward.

Luckily, my house sold relatively quickly, and I found myself in an unfamiliar but very welcome position. The feeling was amazing – knowing that I now had money in the bank that I could use to buy somewhere else. I decided I would like a place a little outside Dublin, preferably with a garden. I started looking at newspapers and auctioneers in a different way. Within a short time I spotted a property that was just an hour's drive from Dublin and seemed to have everything I wanted. Ever since visiting an enchanting walled garden with my grandmother as a child, I had nurtured an ambition to own one. Clondeglass, set in the foothills of the Slieve Bloom Mountains, Co. Laois, an area of the Irish midlands that has some of the most beautiful scenery in the country, had a small house and a walled garden that had once been part of a large estate. The advertisement, though, emphasised that the stone with which the house had been built was valuable and that the house could be knocked down and the stone sold separately. The idea of this happening horrified me and I thought the best thing to do was to take a look.

So one afternoon, I set off with a family member in tow to do just that. We arrived on a beautifully sunny spring morning and my first instinct was to explore the garden. The old gates had completely rotted and in their place was a rough metal and timber structure. Inside, sheep were grazing with their lambs. It was completely overgrown, but there was potential and I knew that I could create a beautiful garden there. The small house was part of the wall. The roof had crumbled in but the stonework was in good condition. The next task was to put in a bid for the property. This I did, but the auctioneer returned within a few days saying there was another bidder and that the owner wanted more money.

This caused me to rethink – I wasn't in the position to go looking for another mortgage, as at that point I was still unemployed. I knew it had to fall within my budget or I'd have to look elsewhere.

I returned, though, to take another look. It was another beautiful day and this time I went inside and walked around. I noticed that the walls, though generally in good condition, were covered in many parts with ivy. The ivy had very thick trunks and had obviously been there for many years. There were nettles growing around the edges and they were very healthy and large, which indicated that the soil quality was good. I searched for traces of old paths without success, but I could see where some old daffodils were growing and also where there had been fruit trees. I looked inside the house and saw that the interior was in very poor condition. The floor was rotting, the small stairway had collapsed and you could see the sky through the roof. But this didn't deter me. I could visualise how it could be transformed and turned into a charming, small, one-bedroomed cottage. I resolved to put in a revised offer, but within a week I was told I had been outbid. At that point, I decided it wasn't for me. I needed to start looking elsewhere.

Three months passed, but I found nothing with the charm and atmosphere of Clondeglass. By coincidence, one day I was driving in the area with my father. As we passed by, I noticed that the 'for sale' sign was still up. What I had been told about it being sold obviously was not true. So I asked my father if he would represent me the following week and make enquiries anew. He did this, put in a bid on my behalf and secured the little house and walled garden as well as some land outside

the walls. Within a few weeks all the paperwork was completed and I was the owner of Clondeglass. The feeling of excitement and the thrill of owning my own walled garden was a dream come true. Though I knew there was a huge amount of work to be carried out, I felt prepared and ready for the task.

Overleaf Amongst the vivid red *Crocosmia* 'Lucifer', which is planted in swathes, are *Allium* seedheads. Next to the *Crocosmia* is the purple *Verbena rigida*, which is underplanted with a pale, lavender-coloured perennial wallflower. Alongside this is the salmon pink *Potentilla x hopwoodiana*.

Rescuing Clondeglass

The first owners were the Pimm family – prominent, highly regarded Quakers, who moved into Clondeglass in the 1700s. From the few records available and also talking to local people, it appears their estate covered an extensive area in the region of 1,000 acres.

In the early 19th century, the Pimm family built a new house more suited to the scale of the estate. It had an adjoining walled garden which employed many people from the surrounding area, including the family of Peter Dobbin. In the late 1970s, the last of the Pimm family died and the property was divided up by the Land Commission. Peter Dobbin's family acquired a portion that included the main house, the walled garden, stables, farmland and woodland.

In Victorian times, it was not unusual for a large estate to employ at least three gardeners per acre, so with Clondeglass being just over an acre in size it is likely that in its heyday the garden would have been extensively planted and cared for. Certainly some thought went into its construction and position, as the walls are made of sandstone and the corners are curved. The whole garden is also on a gentle slope, as was traditional, meaning the south side is exposed to the sun, helping to warm it up.

Knowing that I was going to create the garden of my dreams, the first thing I checked was the drainage. There was evidence of original drains but they were very badly dilapidated. So I employed contractors to create a new drainage system. This meant bringing in digging machinery and excavating to create the perfect drainage system for the garden, all of which happened very quickly. I then sat down with pen and paper and sketched out a rough plan on a sheet of tracing paper showing how I wanted the garden to look. I still have this, and the main structure of the garden has ended up being surprisingly close to that early drawing. I was using my experience of having visited many walled gardens, both around the country and abroad. I was keen for the garden to have a traditional look, so the first task was to lay out the central paths, one running up the centre and the other across the middle, dividing the garden into four large quarters, the way walled gardens have been laid out for several hundred years. Then I set about creating an outer path that would link all of this together. This path ran 4.6m (15ft) out from the wall, all around the garden. I could immediately see a structure starting to form.

While this work was going on, I realised that I would need my own water supply so, again, I hired contractors. I remember the day that a man came and doused the garden. He found a spot just outside the wall on the upper right-hand side and announced that this was where the well was to be dug. A large machine arrived and, after drilling for 66m (216ft), they hit water. The local stone is sandstone and I was advised that the well would have to be lined or it could all crumble and fall in. Then the first water was brought up from the well – beautiful, crystal-clear water that had obviously been filtered on its journey down from the mountains. I learnt that I would never run out of water and that there would always be a supply for whatever I wanted to grow. It was a very satisfying feeling.

Making the Cottage Habitable

Below The cottage with a new window, but before the old timber doors had been selected.

Right Newly painted, with the ornamental barge boards and rooster weather vane in place.

Next, I turned my attention to the little house. I had some good friends who had also restored properties, and they came to look. I was advised to take the roof down and reconstruct it. I did this carefully and managed to save half of the original slate. Being keen to maintain the integrity of the property, I took some of the slate and was able to source salvaged identical slate, with which I covered the other half of the roof. New gutters had to go into place and then a new floor inside, with a small stairway to the upper storey. Some of the walls had to be mended but, luckily, the chimney and fireplaces were intact and in good condition.

I remember standing back and looking at the cottage after the roof had been restored and realising that I could add some more charm to it by including ornamental barge board around the edges. I started looking everywhere in the vicinity. One day I went to Portlaoise and looked at the barge boards on the buildings at the train station. They were exactly the kind of thing I had in mind. So I employed Gavin Duff, a carpenter from Northern Ireland, to make these boards and he made a sample that I liked. He then set about putting this in place and, at the same time, he created a small porch from the garden into the house using salvaged timber from an old church. The finished effect was very pleasing.

That May, I visited the Chelsea Flower Show and, while there, I spotted the perfect colour for Clondeglass. On investigation, I found that it was a Farrow & Ball paint called 'Teresa's Green', which I knew would be available at home. When everything was in place, I painted the woodwork throughout the house and garden, both exterior and interior. At this stage, I still needed an attractive door to lead into the garden through the porch. I was able to buy a piece of stained glass from a salvage company. I was delighted with this as the house had a small remnant of stained glass in the upper window, which had completely rotted, so I felt I was putting something back in place. This stained glass added a touch of magic and the setting sun shines through it, illuminating the downstairs room. Suddenly there was a feeling of completeness.

Finally, a few smaller details were added, such as the weather vane, which I had purchased many years earlier with the cottage in mind. It's a rooster, and I remember spending many hours at a friend's kitchen table gilding it – a slow, laborious task but one that transformed the vane from the plain and ordinary into something eye-catching. I looked at it closely the other day to see that, after ten years, it needs a little work to restore it back to its original condition. I was very surprised that it had lasted so well for so long.

CREATING BEAUTIFUL
Borders

Clondeglass

As a child, I visited the walled garden at Johnstown Castle with my grandmother and was struck with its beauty. I also admired the walled garden at Glenveagh Castle in Donegal. Now, with Clondeglass, I had my own special place, and the space that I had always dreamed of. I had the opportunity to expand my range of plants and grow whatever I wanted. A walled garden provides important shelter and I could take advantage of this. This gave me a great sense of freedom. The thrill was amazing. I could also indulge my passion for roses, a passion that stemmed from childhood and seems always to have been with me. I enjoy not just their colour but also their wonderful scent, and have spent many years admiring roses in other people's gardens. Now, though, I had the space to grow my own.

The stunning tiger lily *Lilium lancifolium*, with the exotic foliage of *Canna* 'Durban' and the bronze-coloured *Crocosmia x crocosmiiflora* 'Solfatare' in front. Behind, to the left, is *Buddleja davidii* 'Black Knight'. On the right is *Eupatorium*, better known as Joe Pye weed.

The East Border

When planting a border, there are three things to always keep in mind. Firstly, scale and height. It may seem obvious, but larger, taller plants need to go at the back and smaller ones at the front. Secondly, colour – specifically what colours will work with those next to and close to them? Thirdly, seasons. Ideally, you should aim always to have things of interest throughout the seasons, from early to late.

Before I did anything at Clondeglass, I planned how I wanted the garden arranged. In my mind, I saw large swathes and drifts of plants, all interlocking with each other. I was keen for the borders to look good in any given month of the year. First, though, I needed to put edging on the borders so I could condition the soil. My father and his friend, Ray, came up with the idea of using boards from the local sawmill, C.J. Sheeran.

These were decking boards that had been fully treated and they made ideal edging, giving structure to the beds. This enabled the soil to be cultivated with well-rotted manure kindly provided by my neighbours, the Bennetts, and with calcified seaweed and other organic materials. Then the fun started. With the help of six gardening friends, the planting began. Because Clondeglass was on such a large scale, I ordered quantities of many favourite plants from Irish wholesale nurseries. Interplanted with these were key focal plants, such as the variegated *Aralia elata*, an occasional specimen rose, a pair of large specimen *Butia* and a few outdoor *Schefflera*. Gradually, it all started to fit together like a jigsaw, right down to the smallest plants such as primulas and small bulbs.

Left The East border with ivy partially removed from the walls and spring plants and bulbs settling in before the paths are completed.

Below An earlier view of the East border, where the ivy on the walls has not been trimmed, looking across a bed of potatoes. The obelisks are now used to support either runner beans or sweet peas.

Another early view of
Clondeglass, taken from
the cottage, looking
across to the East border.
It shows the path system
that divides the garden
and also the polytunnel.

The West Border

The West border leads from the main double gates into the garden and up to the cottage. As I now had the freedom to include the large plants that, up to this point, had only featured in my dreams, I planted four large palms with a pair of *Butia* on each side at one end and a pair of *Trachycarpus* further down.

The size of the border – it's 4.5m (15ft) across – also allowed me to indulge my interest in magnolias, and on both sides of the path are two *Magnolia* x *loebneri* 'Leonard Messel'. These are neat, tidy plants that give a great display in late spring, when they are covered in beautiful, soft pink flowers. They act as excellent sentinels to the start of each border. These borders have been planted with several other magnolias, including *M.* 'Black Tulip' and *M. denudata* 'Yellow River'. At the back, on the left-hand side, is planted a yew hedge. I used small plants and spaced them about 30cm (1ft) apart. The hedge has grown slowly, and the intention is for it to create a division from the rest of the garden and also to add a little extra shelter for the plants growing in that area. It will be easy to maintain and the dark colour will help to set off the paler flowering plants that grow in front of it.

Top The magnolia 'Star Wars'.

Far left Looking towards the main double gates into the garden, showing the West border containing the purple foliage of a red banana plant, blue agapanthus and yellow crocosmia. The *Crocosmia* 'Lucifer' and magnolia are not yet in flower. You can also clearly see the curved corners, which is an unusual feature in a walled garden.

Left The border leading up to the cottage, planted with dwarf, cream-coloured tulips on the left and purple alliums on the right.

The border only a few months later, with planting well underway. The terracotta lattice urns, handmade in Co. Wexford by Kiltrea, are positioned on stones for extra drainage and graduate in size from large to small, to fool the eye into thinking the border is longer than it is.

Both the West border and the Long border have been planted with a wide range of flowering and foliage plants, to create as much interest throughout the four seasons as possible. For summer impact, I used *Crocosmia* 'Lucifer', which settled in extremely well and bulked up, working perfectly in large flowing drifts. The fiery red against its bright green foliage creates fantastic drama in the border. Another plant that thrives here is the tiger lily. I planted several groups and over many years these multiplied. After settling in, they now reach between 2–2.4m (7–8ft) in height and can be seen from all over the garden. A plant that associated extremely well here is the gorgeous mauve-coloured *Verbena bonariensis*, which is interplanted through this vivid orange. In one area underneath this display are planted rich, citron-yellow *Crocosmia* x *crocosmiiflora* 'Solfatare', with smoky bronze foliage. About three-quarters of the way up on each side are *Rhus typhina* 'Tiger Eye'. This has sumptuous cut leaves of golden yellow, and as the foliage emerges on young stems they are a light fluffy salmon pink in colour. This non-spreading variety has turned out to be a plant that I now never want to be without.

Nearby are planted agapanthus. The sapphire blue flowers contrast beautifully with the golden yellow of the *Rhus* foliage. One year, I added vibrant rich pink dahlias, which created a jewel-like effect in that combination. Sadly, I was not able to keep this particular variety going, but always have the option of recreating this display. A perennial that has worked very well close by is *Eupatorium*, commonly known as the Joe Pye weed. This is tall-growing, up to 1.5m (5ft), with a mass of small pink flowers in summer that attract butterflies. I can recall, one summer, counting six different types of butterfly on the plant at the same time. Towards the front of this display, I have tried several times to grow *Verbena rigida*. A rich, purple-flowered, low-growing plant, it creates a fantastic impact when grown together in clumps. Unfortunately,

I have not been able to sustain it, and I put this down to the wet Irish winters – although nothing compares with the horrific winter we had a number of years ago when I lost my *Butia* palms and many 'borderline hardy' plants. To my amazement, however, that particular winter didn't manage to kill the banana plant, which grows at the far end of this border up near the cottage. This has survived for many years, with just a little mulching in winter and removing of dead leaves after frost. It grows like an exotic-foliaged perennial plant but never flowers, though its sheer size makes it a striking feature plant in that corner.

As the eye is led along this border, the path gently narrows, adding to the illusion of it being longer than it actually is. The flowering plants at the edge of the border are changed seasonally. Clumps of red tulips are planted in late spring, which are repeated for visual effect. For the same impact later in the year, I use *Dahlia* 'Bishop of Llandaff', with its bright red flowers and dark foliage. This creates colour from summer until the first frost. Also for interest along the edge of the border there are small groups of interesting seasonal plants: primroses (preferably named varieties), a clump of *Ophiopogon planiscapus* 'Nigrescens', and an occasional grouping of small dwarf grasses. The borders are planted in tiers, allowing spaces for plants to come into show as others fade.

Far left A flourishing banana plant, *Musa basjoo*. To the left is a purple cordyline, and to the right a *Buddleja davidii* 'Nanho Blue'.

Left Verbena bonariensis visited by a red admiral butterfly.

Overleaf The West border. In the foreground, from the left, is a dahlia, allium seedheads and *Euphorbia*. The silver-leaved plant is *Ealeagnus pungens* 'Quicksilver'. The tall plant to the right is *Verbena bonariensis*.

Dividing Areas

The West border leads into a small enclosed area, which acts as a divider between two differently planted areas. The enclosed area is surrounded on three sides by yew hedging and on the fourth side by a wall. On the opposite side, in front of the yew, is a large magnolia called *M*. 'Star Wars', which was planted in memory of a gardening friend, Anna Nolan. It produces big pink-flushed flowers in May. Below this is a range of smaller plants including *Crocosmia* 'Rowallane Yellow', which has rich golden yellow flowers in the summer, and a few interesting Japanese peony cultivars that are slowly developing and showing promise. Flat on the ground in front of these plants is a large stone figure, a copy of a dancer from Angkor Wat in Cambodia. This was purchased many years ago, and I have plans

to incorporate it into a small pool where water can gently spill down the figure into the pond. A large garden bench, painted in the same colour as the cottage woodwork, acts as a focal point here and is visible from both borders.

This area gives way to a pair of borders that continue right up to the cottage door. These borders are planted primarily with roses, both modern and old-fashioned. The borders are edged with *Nepeta* 'Six Hills Giant', which I allow to spill out onto the path. When in full flower, this creates a magnificent display. Several geraniums have been added, including *G*. 'Rozanne' with its rich, violet-blue, white-centred blossoms, as well as *G. psilostemon*, which has vivid cerise flowers and jet-black centres. Behind this row, I add seasonal bulbs such as *Tulipa* 'Angélique', a beautiful early pink double, and *Allium hollandicum* 'Purple Sensation'. All of these colours work extremely well with the range of roses. When planting the roses, I included several clumps of *Rosa* 'Bonica'. This repeat-flowers very well and creates a wonderful summer show. At the end of the right-side border, close to the cottage doorway, I have planted *Daphne bholua* 'Peter Smithers'. I placed it here so I could enjoy its wonderful scent in the early months of the year. Behind this is *Clematis viticella* 'Mary Rose', a wonderful and ancient variety, which produces lots of small double purple flowers. I have tried to train this several times, but without success. After pruning each year, it insists on growing up into nearby plants. This creates a very attractive display, as its colour and shape are very complementary to the surrounding old rose varieties.

Far left A yew hedge enclosing hyacinths and daffodils. The area beyond, with the obelisks, is now planted with roses.

Left The terracotta sphinx, sitting in the middle of the path, works as a focal point.

Overleaf Either side of the path are two *Taxus baccata* 'Irish Yew' plants, which have an upright, narrow-growing habit and are being trained into double globes. Edging the path is *Nepeta* 'Six Hills Giant'.

Points of Interest

Above A small terracotta lattice urn planted with the dramatic leaves of *Canna* 'Durban' and summer flowers, including the begonia 'Bonfire'.

Right A Pope's urn in front of the cottage, used as a focal point.

While laying out the first border and the rose garden area, it seemed to be a good idea to create an intermission between them. This is acheived by planting the surround on each side with yew, developing topiaries to act as sentinels. On the wall grows a fan-trained fig called *Ficus* 'Digitata', which has extraordinarily beautiful leaves that are divided like fingers on a hand. For many years in this spot there was a large terracotta Egyptian sphinx seated in the middle, which acted as a focal point. It has since been replaced with a garden bench, which serves as a perfect spot to stop and take a break. It also helps to prevent you seeing the full way along, creating the interest of not knowing what's to come.

To continue with the terracotta theme of the sphinx, I purchased some handmade Irish terracotta pots from Kiltrea Bridge Pottery in Gorey, Co. Wexford. I bought these in pairs – two large, two medium and two small. The large are used at the beginning, medium midway and the smaller ones at the end, again helping the illusion of distance on the path. The contents of these pots changes annually and sometimes seasonally. Bulbs and/or bedding plants are a favourite.

I also use blue-and-white Oriental jars and seats for visual impact. The containers don't have drainage, so couldn't be planted. Instead, I placed plants in large pots in them, which are raised up off the base so the plants don't get soaked all the time. In winter, the pots have to be turned over to drain, as any water in them could freeze and crack them. During one particularly bad winter they also needed to be covered with bubble wrap, to protect them from frost and snow. I'm glad to say that, seven years later, they are still all intact.

Lomandra confertifolia Ssp. *rubiginosa*

A blue-and-white ceramic seat.

ACHIEVING COLOUR
Throughout the year

Clondeglass

Spring

Spring is one of the most exciting times of year. It's that stage when new life begins to sprout and appear in the garden. Buds are swelling and beginning to open, and there's always a sense of new growth when you find one of those rare warm spring days. It's a favourite time to walk around the garden and to enjoy many exciting things that are coming into growth. Everything from the new buds developing on a magnolia through to watching the unfolding petals of a primula or a crown imperial bring a special joy that is found only in the garden on a spring morning.

Narcissus 'Brackenhurst' with dark purple 'Queen of Night' and pink 'Dreamland' tulips.

Crown Imperials *(Fritillaria imperialis)*

Above Fritillaria imperialis

Right The East border in spring. As well as crown imperials, there are narcissi, the hyacinth 'Woodstock' and Barnhaven cowichan primulas.

I am always happy when I discover that a plant has an interesting mythology or story to tell. This is the case with one of my favourite bulbs, the crown imperial. If you have ever seen a crown imperial, you'll know that the bell-shaped flowers hang in a cluster. But very few people stop to look inside, and this is where its legendary story comes in. If you take a peep, you'll see a cluster of shining nectar droplets, and if you tap the flower the droplets will fall like tears. The story goes that the crown imperial grew near Calvary, and when Christ was on his way to his crucifixion the proud flowers didn't hang their heads. But ever since, they permanently hang their heads with tears of shame.

As the name 'crown imperial' suggests, it is a spectacularly impressive flowering bulb, which I have grown many times over the last 30 years. The splendour of the flower is that each cluster is crowned with a tuft of green leaves. Most varieties reach 1m (3ft) high. They are native to the foothills of the Himalayas and surrounding areas. They flower here from late April into May.

When I started to develop the walled garden at Clondeglass, crown imperials were high on the list of bulbs to be planted. I bought the regular orange-flowered crown imperial from a local garden centre and planted it close to the wall in a bed which had been well dug and had good drainage. The result was a spectacular display, but what really impressed me was that they came back the following year and flowered again without much effort. This indicated that they liked the conditions in Clondeglass and it encouraged me to be a little more adventurous, so I set about hunting for what I knew were named varieties. I searched through the *RHS Plant Finder*, which was extremely helpful in locating individual cultivars. In addition, with a little extra homework, I tracked down a few specialist nurseries in the Netherlands. Between them all, I was able to make up quite a selection of crown imperials – enough to satisfy the collector in me.

I decided that, because they had grown so well, I would plant them in large clumps, so they are now planted in individual groups in my west- and east-facing borders. The preparation for planting was very important. The first priority was to make sure that the soil had perfect drainage. Because I wanted to plant the individual bulbs deeply, I dug a large hole, added sharp grit at the base, and the soil I had removed was mixed with grit and organic compost. The bulbs were then positioned on their sides, as the top of the bulb has a hollow and I was keen to prevent this filling with moisture, which could cause rot. Each bulb was carefully positioned and then soil gently filled back in. At this stage, the bulbs can bruise, so it's important that they're treated with care. The other thing you'll notice is the strong aroma, which I recall being told smelled of female fox. Never having encountered a female fox, I could only take their word for it! I have since been told that the reason for that scent is to discourage the bulbs being eaten by rodents, and that seems to make sense.

Once the planting hole was filled, I put a layer of approximately 2.5cm (1in) of grit on the surface to mark the spot. This helps to protect from accidental disturbance. I also labelled each variety.

While wading through catalogues and searching on the internet, I quickly realised that there were many interesting and very old cultivars to be found. Top of my list were two different variegated forms. The first, *Fritillaria imperialis* 'Argenteovariegata', was planted in a group of 12. This variety is noted for its creamy white variegated leaves, with rich terracotta orange flowers. The second was a little more difficult to find; *F.O.* 'Aureomarginata'. This has pale creamy yellow variegation, which is complemented by orange bells.

I then went looking for a yellow-flowered variety and found *F.O.* 'Maxima Lutea'. This produces the typical large bells, but of a beautiful, rich, deep sulphur-yellow colour. The yellow with the green tuft is very striking, and this variety makes a splendid contrast when planted near to the orange varieties.

On my searches, I came across a crown imperial called 'William Rex'. Before purchasing, I assumed that it was named after William of Orange and guessed that the flowers would be that colour, and that turned out to be the case. They are a dark bronzey orange. Planted near the purple smoke bush *Cotinus coggygria* 'Grace', the combination creates a dramatic impact in the garden and always draws attention.

Still continuing on my search for named crown imperials, I have located several other varieties which I await to see. These include *Fritillaria imperialis* 'Striped Beauty', 'The Premier', and 'Prolifera'. It's said that in ancient times there was a double-flowered variety but I don't believe it is around today.

When I see these wonderful flowers in bloom, and as my collection slowly grows, I can fully understand why the Dutch masters included them so prominently in many of their floral masterpieces. They continue to inspire today.

Left A golden variety, 'Maxima Lutea'.

The silver-variegated variety called 'Argenteovariegata'.

The golden-variegated variety 'Aureomarginata'.

The dark, bronzey orange variety 'William Rex'. In front is *Euphorbia characias*. The tall plant in the middle is *Schefflera* 'taiwaniana', commonly known as the umbrella plant.

Hyacinths

At the age of seven, I remember my teacher, Mr Eager, involving all the class in growing hyacinth bulbs in water on our rather large school windowsills. Each boy was given a number that was placed on the hyacinth glass. My number was 35, and I know there were over 40. We were all given a prepared hyacinth bulb and then told what to do. It was explained exactly what would happen. Over the next six to eight weeks the bulbs began to root. There was a great sense of anticipation in the class with all the boys and this developed into a sense of competitiveness, especially as the shoots started into growth. At last, after what seemed like forever to a young boy, the bulbs started developing their flower buds. The flowers eventually appeared in pink, blue, white and pale yellow and the classroom became filled with rich fragrance. My one was a pale blue. Many years later, when I smelled one again, I instantly remembered my school days in the classroom. It's amazing how scent can transport you back such a long time.

Left The bed that divides the border leading up to the cottage, planted with a variety of hyacinths, including 'Ben Nevis' (white), 'Orange Boven' and 'Woodstock' (see also below), and *Narcissus*.

When I started working on making the garden at Clondeglass, one of the first projects was to collect as many different hyacinth varieties as I could. Alan Shipp, who was then holder of the National Collection of Hyacinth Varieties in the UK, kindly sold me a collection of different old varieties and told me about their history. This world-renowned collector was a font of knowledge. He told me how, in 1753, one grower offered 351 varieties for sale. He also told me how Peter Voorhelm discovered a beautiful white double with a coloured centre to the flower. It was named 'Konig van Groot-brittanje', which translates into 'King of Great Britain'. This started a hyacinth mania which nearly rivalled that of tulips almost 100 years earlier.

'Orange Boven'

'Pink Royal'

'Woodstock'

'Gipsy Princess'

Alan also explained the mythology behind the naming of hyacinth. Apollo and Zephyr, the two sons of the sun god Zeus, were very attracted to the beautiful young man Hyakinthos and began to compete for his friendship. When Apollo threw his spear in the air, the jealous Zephyr blew it off course and it struck Hyakinthos a fatal blow. As the youth lay dying, beautiful blue flowers sprung up from the blood flowing from his body.

With Alan's encouragement and enthusiasm, I set about planting the full length of the cross-path with hyacinths, buying every variety I could find available, including Alan Shipp's special old types. These included a rainbow of colours. Some that stood out were the beautiful double pink 'Chestnut Flower', the deeper pink 'Anna Marie', a delicate soft mauve blue called 'Blue Peter', one the colour of clotted cream called 'Gipsy Princess', a double white called 'Ben Nevis', and the most gorgeous deep navy blue called 'Menelik'. The result was fantastic and when they flowered the air was filled with their glorious scent.

This sweet frangrance has many different notes, including cloves, lavender, rose, and ripe peaches. I managed to sustain the display for many years, but slowly they started to die off, one by one. I particularly regret the loss of 'Orange Queen', a rich salmon orange variety, and also the decline of an almost sky blue form called 'Queen of the Blues'. I put this down to my not dividing them frequently enough as well as the excessive wet weather we had in those particular years. I still grow lots of hyacinths at Clondeglass, but not in the same quantities. Varieties I now have include more readily available cultivars like 'Delft Blue', a magnificent one called 'Woodstock', with burgundy tinges, a yellow named 'City of Haarlem', and a lovely soft pale pink called 'Lady Derby'.

There is a rare black hyacinth called 'Midnight Mystique'. Three bulbs of this changed hands for the astonishing sum of £150,000 and it has only recently become available from Thompson & Morgan.

The national collection grown by Alan Shipp contained in excess of 170 different varieties, both double and single, and in a wide range of colours. He collected and saved many of the older types in Europe before they were completely abandoned and forgotten.

Hyacinths are easy-to-grow bulbs in the garden. They are best planted in late summer or autumn at approximately 10cm (4in) deep. Make the planting hole 15cm (6in) and add a little horticultural grit to help create some extra drainage. Hyacinth are not fussy about soil, and once they have good drainage and are planted in sun, they are generally happy. I use high-potassium pelleted organic fertiliser to encourage extra blooms.

Hyacinths look spectacular when planted in large blocks. They're great in tubs and containers, not just for the fantastic scent but also for the lovely subtlety of colours from different varieties. It's even worthwhile planting a row, if you have space in your vegetable garden, to use them as cut flowers. They last for a long time in water and help to bring the garden indoors.

'Ben Nevis'

'Chestnut Flower'

Overleaf The West border leading up to the cottage in spring, with tulips and *Narcissus* in bloom.

'Menelik'

'Anna Marie'

Tulips *(Tulipa)*

In late spring and early summer each year, Clondeglass comes to life with a blaze of colourful tulips. For best impact, I plant them in large clumps. This also helps them to support each other as the stems of tall varieties can be broken by strong winds.

Tulips are divided into three flowering groups: early, mid and late spring. When you purchase the bulbs, this is usually mentioned on the packaging. Tulips are also divided into different flowering types such as lily-flowered, early doubles, parrot, and Darwin tulips.

Tulips have been grown for hundreds of years and during the 1700s there was a huge craze for tulips in Holland called Tulipomania. At this time, tulips exchanged hands for enormous sums of money and it was not unheard of for a house to be exchanged for one bulb. Striped tulips were very highly prized and today these are known as Rembrandt tulips. Great Dutch masters often included tulips in their artworks as symbols of great wealth. Today, tulip breeding continues and the bulbs are sold all over the world.

Each year at Clondeglass I like to try new varieties along with many traditional cultivars. I usually seek the advice of Thomas Quearney of Mr Middleton Garden Shop in Dublin, who travels each year to Holland to purchase the best-quality bulbs. A few years ago, I decided to plant up a large oval flowerbed that flanks both sides of the central path. While doing a little research, I discovered that the late, great gardener Christopher Lloyd of Great Dixter loved the tulip 'Queen of Sheba'. This is an exquisite lily-flowered tulip with bright red pointed petals edged with golden yellow. I have interplanted this with the tulips 'Pink Delight' and 'Apricot Beauty'. Because I was keen to have the

bulbs repeat flower for several years, I planted each bulb especially deep, to at least 20cm (8in). I find that by planting the bulb deeper it usually discourages it from producing smaller offsets and, as a result, the energy stays in the bulb longer for flowering. By doing this, along with good soil preparation and always allowing the tulip foliage to die back naturally, I get a second and often a third flowering from the planting. After planting I covered the exposed soil with a low-growing grass seed. This was primarily to discourage weeds. It has worked extremely well and only requires an occasional cutting when the tulips have died back. In flower, the overall effect was most attractive, reminding me of a Flemish tapestry.

I also grow tulip favourites including the double peony tulip 'Angélique', which is a gorgeous pink flower and, when fully open, resembles an old-fashioned herbaceous peony. Another great favourite in the garden is the lily-flowered tulip 'Westpoint'. This has elegant rich yellow pointed petals set on tall stems, making this tulip very striking. In total contrast, another tulip called 'Queen of Night' is a wonderful classic of the deepest burgundy colour.

Left 'Angélique' tulips along the edge of the border in front of the nerine house. Underneath the tulips is *Nepeta*, which is yet to come into flower. Behind is a white dicentra.

Overleaf Left, the double tulip 'Uncle Tom', underplanted with white pansies and white forget-me-nots. Right, a purple parrot tulip.

'Angélique'

From a distance, it can give the illusion of being black: it's very beautiful and very striking. In another part of the garden, I have a favourite red-and-white tulip with a very different shape. This is an early double called 'Carnaval de Nice', and each flower looks like a bowl of raspberry ripple ice cream. I often grow more of this variety to use as a cut flower or to grow en masse in a container, where it can be very impressive.

There are hundreds of tulips to choose from and growers and breeders have divided them into many horticultural divisions. The colour range is wide and wonderful and recently, in a French garden, I came across a brown tulip called 'James Wild'. This particular colour may not appeal to everyone but I imagine flower arrangers would find it a very useful and unusual colour to include in an arrangement.

The brilliant red-flowered variety called 'Ile de France' is planted in groups along one of the borders, and when it comes into flower your eye is drawn along the full length, creating an elongated effect and giving the impression that the border is longer than it really is.

I plan to use the red-and-white parrot tulip 'Estella Rijnveld' in the same way along the border. This tulip produces serrated and jagged red-and-white flowers. When grown in a group, it creates a flamboyant display. I have always liked parrot tulips, but realise that when in flower they take centre stage and can dominate. Not suitable for a windowbox, for example. A little thought needs to go in to where you plant them. With this in mind, the display can be very rewarding. Parrot tulips offer a great array of colours and with their wonderful shape, they really stand out.

I often buy and plant my tulips late in the season, sometimes even planting them as late as early January. Providing the bulbs are firm and in good condition they will grow well. It also means that I can avail of bargains as, at that time, garden centres and hardware stores are often selling off bulbs at a special price. These are often used in rows in the vegetable garden and make superb late-spring cut flowers. The display is always well worth waiting for.

'Queen of Night'

'Flaming Parrot'

'Flaming Spring Green'

'Huis Ten Bosch'

Chatham Island Forget-me-not *(Myosotidium)*

Above and below right
The blue form.

Over my decades of gardening, I have met many gardening experts from all over Ireland, often on my travels around the country giving gardening talks. One plant that constantly crops up in conversation, usually with gardeners in the know, is the Chatham Island forget-me-not. This magnificent plant always captures attention because of its exotic large, shiny foliage, and the panicles (compound clusters of flowers on a stem) of fantastic china blue flowers. Each individual flower looks as if it has been hand crafted from the best porcelain.

This short-lived perennial has a reputation for being tricky and has been lost by even the most skilled of growers, but this does not deter them from trying again. It is a glorious plant officially known as *Myosotidium hortensia*. It is now endangered in its native habitat, where it has been vulnerable to many different types of pressure, including grazing, weeds, and marran grass. It grows in the remote Chatham Islands, which belong to New Zealand. The Chatham Islands are the first inhabited land in the world to greet the dawn each morning. This exquisite plant grows on rocky outcrops and coastal cliffs and is sometimes found on the edges of forests, just at the beach line, where it is happy in the midst of kelp and paua shells.

I am also lucky to grow the rare white form. I recently discovered from one of the New Zealand government conservation websites that the last flowering white plant has gone and is now lost from the wild.

The leaves of the Chatham Island forget-me-not are huge and glossy, and the panicles of exquisite blue flowers are worth close inspection, being a lovely shade of china blue, fading to white at the edge. They look like forget-me-nots on steroids. They are large without being flamboyant, and when in full flower they have a beautiful grace about them. In their native habitat, the plants grow into clumps which can be over 1m (3ft) in diameter. Their usual flowering time is in September/October in the Southern Hemisphere. They reproduce readily from fresh self-set seeds and this is how the plant has become available in our nursery trade.

As I write this in spring, my white-flowered plant is showing flower buds. I'll mind these like gold and collect the seed when it's ripe. I grow my plants by starting them off in large pots using a good-quality peat-based compost. I do my best to keep them evenly moist, as they resent drying out. I use a seaweed-based fertiliser when planting out and give each plant a little dressing of calcified seaweed to remind them of home.

The beautiful foliage.

The white variety, *Myosotidium hortensia* 'Alba'.

As mentioned, they are not long-lived perennials so it's very important to let each plant set seeds. I usually see bumblebees around the flowers doing their job of pollination. If you let the seeds ripen, you'll see the green nut-like capsule turn brown. Sow immediately, as they do not keep very long and will not stay fresh. When freshly sown, you just lightly cover them and they will germinate quite quickly.

In Clondeglass, I grow my plants in a group, forming a small colony. They are placed in light shade with no competition from other plants and, when planting, I make sure to incorporate plenty of organic fertiliser, especially one that I know contains seaweed extract.

Several very good examples of this flower can be seen in some of my favourite Irish gardens. In the enclosed area at Glenveagh Castle, Co. Donegal, Head Gardener Seán Ó Gaoithín grows a wide array of these plants to perfection. He maintains that they grow well in some Donegal gardens, where they're fed on seaweed, and he also mentioned a garden in Scotland that he admires called Inverewe, which is right beside the sea, where they grow extremely well. And in Co. Wicklow at Kilmacurragh, Head Gardener Seamus O'Brien looks after these stately plants. Seamus, like many other gardeners, admits that he finds myosotidium difficult to maintain. Both of these gardens are open to the public.

I always have a feeling of excitement when I see this wonderful plant coming into bloom.

Primulas *(Primula)*

On a recent trip through the Irish countryside, on my way to Donegal, I was delighted to see our wild native primrose growing abundantly in banks and hedgerows by the roadsides. Their beautiful soft pale yellow colour is always a joy to see.

Above Barnhaven polyanthus, 'Amethyst Cowichan'. Cowichans are characterised by intense colours that continue solidly into the centre of the flower, unrelieved by the normal yellow eye.

Right The unusual, green-flowered polyanthus 'Francesca'.

For as long as I can remember, primroses have been part of my life. My grandmother and mother both loved them and grew many different types in their gardens. At Clondeglass, just outside the east wall, there is a walk along a bank that was originally planted with hazel for coppicing. This bank has, over many years, developed a wild, natural look and now has some very old wild primroses. In bright spots, there's also an odd cowslip. Seeing these doing well encouraged me to grow primulas in the walled garden and I set about collecting as many old Irish cultivars as I could. The *RHS Plant Finder*, in particular, was a great help. Soon I had located several reliable sources and started to build up a good range.

Bob Brown of Cotswold Garden Flowers was especially helpful. Bob grows a wide range of primulas, including many old Irish types. I have also been delighted to speak to Ireland's leading primrose breeder, Joe Kennedy, who has spent over 30 years developing and breeding new strains of primrose, two of which have been planted at Clondeglass. Both have bronze foliage and are extremely strong-growing. 'Inisfree' has a lovely rich ruby-coloured flower and 'Drumcliffe' is a pale shell pink. The dark leaves set off the flowers of both varieties extremely well. These are only two, with many more to come.

Ireland was famous for its primrose cultivars in the 1800s right through into the 1960s. Sadly, most of these have been lost to cultivation. Varieties like 'Irish Sparkler', a hose-in-hose (a flower sitting within a flower, now quite rare) of crimson red with a yellow centre is one that is no longer found. The variety 'Garryarde Guinevere', a beautiful primrose with bronze-tinted foliage and pink flowers, is still sometimes available, as is another old variety of Irish origin, 'Kinlough Beauty'. It has a polyanthus habit (has stems carrying the flowers). The colouring is a salmon pink with a cream stripe down the centre of each petal. It originated from a Mr Johnston's garden in Kinlough, Co. Donegal. I also grow at Clondeglass an old Irish cultivar called 'Tawny Port', which has a beautiful port wine-coloured flower set against dark, bronzy foliage. It's said that this originated in the west of Ireland. 'Julius Caesar' has claret-coloured flowers and bronzy green foliage. This is one of many primulas bred by Miss Winifred Wynne at her home in Avoca, Co. Wicklow in the 1940s and 50s. Sadly, most of her introductions are now lost to cultivation, but I was delighted to be given a plant of 'Julius Caesar' from Janet Wynne, a cousin of the redoubtable Miss Wynne.

About 20 years ago, I grew a green-flowered primrose more as a curiosity than a great beauty. It had very poor vigour and, despite lots of good care, I eventually lost it. So when I came across a green polyanthus called 'Francesca' at Cotswold Garden Flowers, I had to try it. The flowers are a beautiful shade of jade green and the plant is strong-growing and vigorous. Each flower has

a pale yellow central eye and flowers from March until July. According to Bob, this primula was discovered by Francesca Darts on a bedding scheme on a traffic roundabout in Surrey, British Columbia, Canada. The plant has grown extremely well for me and I have been able to divide it and try it in several different places. Close by, I grow another very attractive primula, a gold-laced polyanthus type. Each flower has the darkest mahogany red with the individual petals edged or laced with gold, creating a stunning effect. It flowers from February until mid June each year. I grow it in a spot where other herbaceous perennials will provide shade for mid to late summer.

Along the edge of the newest east-facing border at Clondeglass are planted many groups of Barnhaven primroses and polyanthus. These include Indian reds, which have varying shades of vermillion, scarlet, crimson and bright reds. I am also pleased with another strain from Barnhaven called 'Spice Shades'. These colours include ginger, cinnamon, coffee and all spice. In total contrast, I also grow 'Harbour Lights' and this provides interesting shades of smokey apricot, salmon reds and pastel reds. The Barnhaven colour range is outstanding, and not only are plants available, but seeds are too. I have tried their 'Desert Sunset' range, which includes a mix of coral, salmon, shrimp, champagne, prawn red, begonia pink, apricot and burnt orange shades.

At Clondeglass, I have found primroses easy to grow in well-prepared soil that does not dry out and into which plenty of organic matter has been incorporated before planting. Primulas have a low tolerance for extremes, preferring moisture in a bright spot. I have found it

useful to divide plants every two or three years as this can revive them.

Another way of guaranteeing vigorous, strong plants is to grow plants from seed. This is not difficult if you follow a few simple rules. Firstly, find fresh seed from a good, trusted source. Next, purchase the best-quality seed compost available. Fresh compost from a reliable source is vital. If a large quantity of one variety is needed, it is better to sow the seeds in trays. Pots give you more control over growing individual varieties. Make sure your containers are clean. After filling with compost, sprinkle the seed onto the surface. Gently press the seed so it's in full contact with the compost, but do not cover with compost, as it needs light to germinate. Each sowing should be labelled with the variety name and date of sowing. Make sure to use an indelible marker! Then water. My method is to fill a clean watering can in advance, allowing it to reach room temperature before pouring it into a container and then standing the trays/pots in the water. Avoid pouring water on the top as this can dislodge seeds, bury them deeply and prevent them germinating. By standing the pots in water for around 20 minutes, you will eventually notice the surface of the compost becoming damp. Remove from the water, allow the pots to drain and cover them with either clear plastic or glass. If you have a propagator, that can be used instead. This is a good way to keep moisture at the right level for germination.

Germination usually takes up to 14 days. When the seedlings develop, let them grow several leaves before lifting and dividing. Carefully pot them into individual 10cm (3in) flower pots. This is a very economical way of growing lots of plants.

'Drumcliffe', an Irish primrose.

'Jack in the Green', a primrose with a ruff of leaves in which the flower sits.

Barnhaven polyanthus 'Blue Cowichan'

Barnhaven polyanthus 'Red Indian'

Tree Peonies *(Paeonia)*

Peonies are among the most regal flowering plants I grow. For centuries, peonies have been grown in China and Japan. The traditional herbaceous peony, which goes underground in winter to emerge the following spring, is probably the most familiar type of peony grown in our gardens today. Along with these is another type known as the tree peony, also loved in Chinese and Japanese culture. The tree peony is more shrubby in its growth, producing branches above ground. Deciduous, it loses its leaves in winter, leaving woody stems.

Above P. suffriticosa.

Left 'Duchesse de Mornay', another *P. suffriticosa.*

Tree peonies are impossible to compare with other shrubby plants, as they can be so exceptional when in full flower that they steal the limelight. I have grown tree peonies over many years, starting with Japanese varieties, which are noted for having longer, more slender growth. The flowers also differ from Chinese tree peonies in having a wider palette of colours. The flowers are not quite as double, because the fashion at the time of their development was for single to semi-double varieties. Chinese tree peonies are often bushier in their growth, and the style and taste was, traditionally, for fully double flowers. Both Japanese and Chinese tree peonies are exquisite, and every effort should be made to accommodate at least one.

In both China and Japan, tree peonies were highly prized by artists, and examples of the flowers appear in paintings, on fabrics, porcelains, and other *objets d'art*. They are also celebrated in poetry, and I always have great pleasure when I read translations of names given to particular varieties in each culture. For example, two Chinese tree peonies that come to mind are named 'Qing Long Wo Mo Chi' (Green dragon lying on a Chinese ink stone) and 'Ying Luo Bao Zhu' (Necklace with precious pearls). And the same tradition of poetic names is also seen in Japan, with names including

'Gunpo-den' (Temple adorned with many flowers) and 'Horakumon' (Invitation to abundant pleasure).

To this day, peonies grown in Japanese gardens are treated with the greatest respect and reverence and this goes beyond simply caring for them. There's an almost spiritual element to growing these glorious plants.

One of my favourite tree peonies is the 'Duchesse de Morny'. This is a very old French variety and remains a popular classic. Grown in many old Irish gardens, and to perfection in Helen Dillon's garden in Dublin, the fully double flowers are a beautiful rose pink colour, slightly darkening towards the centre. They are produced abundantly. I have only recently planted this beauty in my new east-facing border at Clondeglass, where three plants are grouped closely together to create impact. During their first winter, I placed them under Victorian glass cloches to protect their emerging foliage from late frosts. The soil was prepared with organic compost (very well-rotted horse manure), and each bare rooted plant was given some Rootgrow to give them the very best start.

Close by is one of the most beautiful tree peonies I grow. This is one of several raised by the late, great plantsman Sir Peter Smithers. He named it after his wife Dojean in 1988. Crimpled, semi-double, pure white flowers open to reveal a circle of golden stamens with a vivid red heart in the centre. Each petal is splashed with the same glowing red. The flower looks like a skilled artist has been working on painting it. The colour combination is exceptional. The simplicity of the combination can only be described as magnificent.

In complete contrast is *P. suffriticosa* 'Dou Lu'. This Chinese name translates into 'pea green'. It is probably the most unusual of all the tree peonies at Clondeglass. The fully double blooms of this treasured ancient variety open a rich green and slowly turn white.

Another choice tree peony in the collection is *P. rockii*, also known as 'Rock's Variety'. There are two forms of this beautiful plant in cultivation: a British form and an American form. This legendary peony was the holy grail of gardeners for decades. The single flowers are exquisite and open to pure white. Each petal has a central blotch of maroon when fully open. The flowers measure around 16cm (6in) across and the difference between the two types is that the one from these islands has more vigour.

In 1928, the French nursery Lemoine introduced *P.* 'Chromatella'. Said to be a sport of 'Souvenir de Maxime Carnu', I have grown it in my mother's garden since the 1980s and have only recently planted a small specimen at Clondeglass. In my mother's garden, it produces a fantastic annual display. The large double flowers, which can be up to 25cm (10in) across, are yellow and have a very attractive rose-carmine edge.

P. 'Chromatella'

P. suffriticosa 'Rimpo'

It also has a light lemon fragrance. In full flower, it is absolutely stunning and is best planted where it will be seen. The only problem is that the flowers are so heavy that they can hang in rain, so it benefits from a little discreet support.

Tree peonies are hardy plants and, when established, will tolerate cold conditions. However, freezing cold winds can do severe damage to new growth. They can burn the delicate leaves as they unfold. Providing a sheltered spot is important. If worried, use extra protection like horticultural fleece or, with smaller plants, put a cloche in place while the leaves develop and remove it when all signs of cold winds and frost have gone.

The soil is an important element of getting peonies off to the best start. Make sure the ground is well drained and, if not, work on that before planting. They are not fussy plants, providing you have added enough organic matter to the soil in advance. I use a combination of well-rotted homemade compost, a little seaweed meal and, if planting bare root, I'll use Rootgrow for extra help. Plant to the correct level. Whether it was container grown or bare root, you'll see the mark on the stem which should be at soil level. Sometimes tree peonies have been grafted, and it can happen that you get a shoot that doesn't belong appearing from the roots. This must be removed immediately from below soil level to prevent energy being lost from the main plant. This can be simply done with a sharp knife. Also, while plants are establishing, keep an eye out for weeds. These must be removed as they will compete with your plant and tree peonies don't react well to competition.

My annual care for tree peonies is a light mulch in spring and then again in autumn. You can make this up with garden compost, or you can buy a good-quality general organic fertiliser. Try not to overfeed them. Little and often gives better results. Flowering takes a huge amount of energy and, as they're coming into bud, it can be beneficial to give a light liquid feed – something high in potassium, such as an organic tomato feed.

Generally, tree peonies don't require staking, but some of the taller Japanese varieties can benefit from being tied to discreet bamboo canes, as the flowers can become very heavy, especially after rain.

Tree peony 'Black Pirate'

Magnolias *(Magnolia)*

Right 'Leonard Messel'

Overleaf 'Black Tulip'

I have always had a passion for magnolias and never had the room to grow many of them. So when I purchased Clondeglass, it was one of the first plants I wanted to grow. I set about searching for the best varieties available and this took me to many nurseries in Germany, the UK and Ireland.

I can remember as a child standing under a magnolia in full flower and being in total awe. I never forgot that moment. The tree was laden from top to bottom with white tulip-shaped flowers. The mass effect was spectacular and a gentle breeze allowed them to lightly flutter. It was one of those moments that has always stayed with me, so when the opportunity arose to grow my own, I grabbed it with enthusiasm.

I've already planted about 20 different varieties throughout the garden, both inside and outside the walls. They seem to enjoy the soil and the shelter of the garden, which has allowed them to thrive and to flower early. Magnolias have a reputation for being slow to get going, but with my rich soil and sheltered conditions some of them started to flower within just a few years.

Winter is an exciting time, as the plants, which are now large bushes, are laden with fluffy buds – a teaser for the wonderful display to come in spring. On their own, these buds provide a very effective winter display. I sometimes touch them just to feel the sensation of the flower bud, which I know is a promise of the spring display to come. This is always a thrilling moment in the garden.

The planting was very carefully planned and the soil well prepared. I used plenty of organic fertiliser and also included some seaweed. Being conscious of the life within the soil I used EM (see page 158), as I do throughout the garden. I attribute part of the success of these plants to that extra care. The first priority was to find the appropriate space for each plant, making sure there was enough room to allow for the ultimate width of the plants and to plant them far enough away from the walls so that they had plenty of room to develop. Many of them are planted near a yew hedge, which acts as a very good wind break. Also, they get sunlight, which helps their development, and drainage was carefully checked as magnolias do not enjoy sitting in wet soil. I'm lucky that my neutral soil suits them very well. As an extra treat, each magnolia gets an annual mulch in September. This is of well-rotted compost and some organic fertiliser, which works its way into the soil slowly through the winter. As a result, the magnolias don't suffer from drought during the summer and have the right quality and texture of soil around them.

When choosing magnolias, a little homework pays. There's a wide choice available from garden centres and nurseries, and it's very easy to get overwhelmed when trying to find the particular type you want. There are magnolias suited to smaller gardens as there are those that need more room. I am lucky in Clondeglass to have enough space for a combination of different sizes.

The first one I planted on either side of my west border was *Magnolia* x *loebneri* 'Leonard Messel'. This is

among the most widely grown of all magnolia cultivars. It originated in Nymans in Sussex in the 1940s. The plant has an attractive upright habit, making a beautiful sentinel for the beginning of each side of the border, and because of its slow and compact growth, it is suitable for smaller gardens. After many years, it can reach up to 10m (30ft) in height. As I write this in early February it is covered from top to bottom in flower buds. The flowers start to appear from mid-spring and cover the tree in a beautiful pink explosion of colour. Each flower is pink on the outside and white within and emits a delicate fragrance. This particular cultivar is slow-growing and has a reputation of being shy to flower when young. However, in Clondeglass it seems to love the place it's been allocated and has been rewarding me each spring for many years. When in full flower, the overall effect is exquisite and always draws attention.

While hunting for magnolias for Clondeglass, I was aware of the hybridising programme that was going on in New Zealand. Some of the best modern magnolia hybrids have been bred there and have become available to gardeners only in the last few years. One I was aware of, and very excited to find, is called *M.* 'Black Tulip'. As the name suggests, it's a dark-flowered magnolia. This is a New Zealand hybrid raised in the late 1990s – a cross between *M.* 'Vulcan' and *M.* 'Iolanthe'. I discovered that it was a selected seedling from a batch of 150 that were raised from that cross. The colour is an exquisite dark ruby red and the flowers are large and tulip-like. The colour and shape make it one of the most spectacular magnolias in the garden. As it matures and develops, the flowers can darken in colour. It grows strongly and makes a medium, very slender, upright tree. One of the good things about this magnolia is that

it flowers from an early age. 'Black Tulip' is certainly destined to become one of the treasures of the garden.

Not far away from 'Black Tulip', is planted a magnolia called 'Star Wars'. I planted this in memory of a very good gardening friend, Anna Nolan, who was a passionate gardener and inspired me in my early gardening years. She loved flowering plants and I felt that this particular magnolia would be a suitable tribute to her memory. One of the New Zealand hybrids, bred in the 1970s, 'Star Wars' has large flowers measuring around 27cm (11in). The colour is bright pink on the outside and almost pure white within. The huge, blowsy flowers, carried in profusion, create an amazing sight. Again, I'm lucky that it flowered from an early age. While I haven't yet propagated this magnolia myself, I understand that it roots with ease from cuttings, and I'm sure we're destined to see it more widely available.

'Star Wars'

Unfortunately, the blossoms don't carry any scent, but the floral effect is dramatic enough to make up for this.

Further down the border is planted another special magnolia in memory of another good gardening friend, John Cushnie. John was always very generous with his advice and encouragement, but sadly never managed to get to see Clondeglass in person. He remains one of my great gardening inspirations. This magnolia is called *M. denudata* 'Yellow River', a Chinese variety of a species which is reputed to have been grown in China by Buddhist monks over 1000 years ago, making it among the earliest of cultivated garden plants. The variety 'Yellow River' is covered in small, pale, creamy yellow flowers, which have a soft scent. It flowers a little later than some of the other varieties and has been growing very strongly. I have underplanted it with spring-flowering bulbs and have had to watch the plant carefully as the branches are quite brittle. When working around it, I have to take great care. The colour yellow is unusual in magnolias, and this particular variety, when in full flower, adds an unexpected dimension to the display.

At the south end of this border, close to the cottage, is planted one of my all-time favourite magnolias. This beauty is called *M. stellata* 'Jane Platt'. What makes it stand out from others is the gorgeous, sumptuous pink of the flowers. It is in a warm spot close to the wall for shelter, and it settled in very quickly. The flowers have many petals and, when in full bloom, are very eye-catching. The outside is a rich pink with a paler pink centre. In a light breeze, a shimmering effect is created over the plant. Again, I have underplanted it with early-flowering bulbs, such as muscari and white late-flowering daffodils, creating a glorious spring effect.

M. denudata 'Yellow River'

M. x *wieseneri*

Very close to the entrance into the walled garden I have planted a very special magnolia – *M.* x *wieseneri*. This is an ancient plant from Asia and is highly regarded and treasured by gardeners. Very much prized in Japan, it was introduced to these isles in the late 1880s. The flowers are approximately 15cm (6in) across and are especially beautiful. The large single flowers have a central boss of stamens that are pink and red. This contrasts well with the creamy whiteness of the petals. The flowers are upward facing and appear in early summer. *M.* x *wieseneri* has a strong scent that reminds some people of freshly cut pineapple. The wonderful thing is that the scent travels and you are often aware of it before you see the plant. My own plant has not yet flowered, so the anticipation is building for this special moment. It is reputed to flower within three or four years of planting, so I don't have long to wait.

Last year, a very good gardening friend, Carmel Duignan, presented me with a special magnolia which is new to cultivation. This plant, *M. sapanensis*, was discovered in the autumn of 2009 by Nick Macer of Pan-Global Plants, growing on the slopes of Fan Fi Pan mountain in north Vietnam. In 2010 it was officially named as a new species to science. Nick lists it in his own catalogue as the most exciting plant he had for release in 2011. It's noted for its silken leaves, fluffy terminal buds and white leaf backs. The flowers are white, stained purple on the outside, and it's considered to be a small, evergreen magnolia. There's not a lot known about this particular magnolia in cultivation, so I'm being very careful with it. I've given it a very sheltered spot and have covered it with fleece for winter. *M.* x *kewensis* 'Wada's Memory' is a wonderful sight to behold when in full flower. It was a gift to me from garden centre owner Jim Clarke many years ago. It took time to settle in and, with a lot of care, it is now thriving. I planted it in the south-west part of the garden, where it would receive plenty of light. This magnolia has a conical habit and flowers when young. It was named at the University of Washington Arboretum, where it was raised from seed in 1940, the seed having been sent by Mr K Wadda of Japan. The white flowers are 15–17cm (6–7in) wide and, as they develop, the long, narrow petals open completely, giving the impression of the overall flower display being larger than it is. The effect is spectacular and the tree at Clondeglass improves year by year.

Several years ago, a friend sent me a mysterious variegated magnolia, which they claimed came from Russia. It was obviously a *Magnolia grandiflora*, but it had no cultivar name. I received two plants, which I carefully planted in the south-facing part of the walled garden. The foliage is exquisitely splashed with gold flecks, a variegation that appears to be stable. It flowers through summer with large, white flowers which turn cream as they mature. These scented blooms are of an open, globular shape. Following a bad experience with a *M. grandiflora* 'Saint Mary', which died in the bad winter of 2010, I now cover these precious plants with large fleece bags in the winter months to help protect them against cold winds. Gardening friends who have seen this marvellous magnolia have suggested that I might have it named 'Clondeglass Gold'.

Summer

Summer always brings its own special mood. For me, it's often the fragrance caught on the air, from roses beginning to produce their spectacular displays to the first sweet peas that are picked and brought indoors, or the taste of the first ripe tomato. The lengthening days also bring a richer atmosphere to the garden and everything seems to be in full growth. To watch a butterfly visiting from flower to flower or bees collecting nectar from lavender is a great experience. To stop and listen, taking in the magical atmosphere that's uniquely summer, is rewarding and very fulfilling.

Lupins *(Lupinus)*

Right 'Persian Slipper', A compact West Country Nursery lupin, another great favourite for its blue colour. Very desirable.

The first plants I grew from seed were lupins. The seeds had been collected by my grandmother from her garden. My memories of those lupins are still strong. They were tall and there was always the hum of bumblebees around them. The air was full of their peppery sweet scent and the colours were mixed and vibrant. That's when my love affair with these striking plants started. When the flowers were over, there were always a few left in position to set seed while others were carefully removed.

Since the walled garden at Clondeglass has been under restoration, lupins have always been included, but recently I have created a new bed devoted to them. This is a circular bed and in the centre on a post stands a dovecote, designed and created by Peter McDonogh. It is painted the pale green colour used throughout the garden and there is a plan to introduce a pair of black fantail doves later in the summer. Meanwhile, the spot is being prepared for the planting of the lupins. The weeds and grass have been removed and plenty of homemade compost, with some added seaweed, has been rotovated in, creating a lovely, deep and nicely textured soil. The situation is perfect for lupins, as they love sun and good drainage. This circular bed will be surrounded with a box hedge and within this an inner circle of red astrantias, which slugs and snail loathe. Within the astrantias, the lupins will be planted in large blocks, radiating from the central pole that supports the dovecote. I have waited many years to obtain very special lupin cultivars bred by West Country Lupins in Devon. With the help of Cherrie McIlwaine, a good gardening friend from Northern Ireland, the plants made their way to Clondeglass. It may sound like a lot of trouble but these lupin hybrids are, I believe, worth it.

A close up of 'Tequila Flame'.

'Manhattan Lights'. The purple and yellow make this lupin stand out from the crowd. Fantastic.

'Red Arrow' has among the most brilliant coloured flowers in my garden. Can be seen from a long distance, very showy. Wonderful.

'Masterpiece'

In recent years, West Country Lupins have won many gold medals at the Chelsea Flower Show for their fabulous displays, made up of a large selection of their own named hybrids. From this range, I ordered 12 different varieties including: 'Beefeater', with flowers of vibrant, almost pure red; 'Masterpiece', tall, flowering in rich purple with a contrasting orange blotch; 'Manhattan Lights', a beautiful mauve and yellow bicolour; and 'Gladiator', another bicolour with bright orange and yellow flowers. Others in the range include 'Red Rum', 'Polar Princess', 'Desert Sunset' and more.

Apart from slug and snail attack, lupins are prone to their own greenfly, known as lupin aphid. These are larger than regular greenfly and when they lodge on a plant they quickly form dense colonies, often on the flower spikes first, though they can also attack under leaves. If not controlled, your lupins may wilt and in extreme cases they may even die. I have been lucky enough to have avoided this greenfly at Clondeglass, but I am prepared with an organic spray containing pyrethrum (a natural insecticide made from the dried heads of chrysanthemum). It may need to be used several times to ensure their control, but I'll keep it on standby in a cool, protected place for the inevitable event of their arrival. When not controlled, the lupin aphid will usually become so overcrowded that they start to develop winged offspring and these will spread to form new colonies. So vigilance is very important. In autumn, alliums will be added in between the lupins for extra interest next year. These will be effective but will not steal the show when next year's plants come into full bloom. I'm also planning to add a few dozen camassias, which will be divided from well-established plants that are already in the garden.

Roses _(Rosa)_

Above 'Dermot O'Neill', a rose named after me, bred by one of Ireland's leading rose breeders, David Kenny. All proceeds raised from sales of it will go to the Irish Cancer Society.

Right The climbing rose 'Dortmund' in full flower. It is being trained to grow over the arch of the double gates leading into the garden.

Overleaf Left 'Harry Edland', right 'Bonica'

I have always loved growing roses and visiting rose gardens. I have been inspired by some of the world's finest, such as Bagatelle in Paris. This has always been a treat to visit, and there I have seen roses – both old and new varieties – grown beautifully. I always come away feeling recharged and ready to plant more. The same is true of several very good Irish rose gardens, such as the one in Tralee. Perfectly maintained and always pushing boundaries by trying new varieties, it's a garden where you get to see and experience roses close up. Dublin also offers a rose garden of international acclaim at St. Anne's Park, Raheny. Again, it's hard to come away from a rose garden in full flower without the desire to grow ever more varieties.

Clondeglass has given me the opportunity to indulge this passion. The shelter from the high walls provides ideal conditions and, with good soil management, roses do well. I have experimented with roses in different parts of the garden and have been pleased with the results. For me, flower shape and colours are very important when choosing roses, but fragrance is often the deciding factor. I can think of nothing more glorious in the garden than to experience that heady perfume on a summer's evening.

Rosa 'Wild Edric' is a wonderful, tough and beautiful David Austin rose, which has been used in Clondeglass as edging on the path that divides the fruit and vegetable areas. When in full flower, the scent is glorious, and as you walk along you can appreciate its full beauty. It shows very good disease resistance and creates a dense, bushy hedge reaching approximately 1.2m (4ft) in height. Planted approximately 1m (3ft) apart, these roses require minimal pruning, though I deadhead and give a light dressing of organic feed in the growing season. The richly scented flowers are semi-double and a deep, velvety pink. When fully open they reveal golden stamens in the centre. The delicious scent has a touch of cloves, and when you look at the overall effect you can see the influence of one of its parents, _R. rugosa._ I imagine this rose will perform extremely well in coastal areas. The foliage is glossy and disease-free.

'Harry Edland' is possibly the most richly fragrant of all the roses grown at Clondeglass. The scent is superb, sweet and delicious, and carries on the air. The blooms are large and are usually borne three per stem. The colour is a soft mauve-lilac and it is excellent as a cut flower. I believe 'Harry Edland' deserves to be more widely grown. I planted two plants – one on each side of the entrance in my polytunnel. There, they receive good air circulation and protection from rain. This extra protection has helped to develop strong, healthy plants that provide superb cut flowers throughout the summer. This rose repeat flowers through the summer and well into the autumn. Because it provides so much flower, I feed little and often with some organic pellets specially formulated for roses.

Also under the protection of my polytunnel, I grow several other great roses with magnificent scents. 'Louis XIV' never did well for me in the garden, so I made the decision to plant it in the polytunnel to avoid the heavy rain. This has most definitely worked. The plant seems to enjoy the slightly warmer temperature and being in a rain-free position. The flowers are exquisite, deep crimson to the darkest velvet red. Each flower has 25 petals and, when fully open, the petals gently curl back, adding to its beauty and enhancing the colour. Introduced in 1877, long after the demise of the famous Sun King, it is still possible to use your imagination and think of the famous, flamboyant French king holding this sumptuous rose in his hand. It responds well to a little extra care and, while it never produces great quantities of flowers or foliage, what you do get is very special.

Another rose grown close by, and with similar qualities, is 'Empereur du Maroc'. This French rose was raised in 1858 and the blooms are of a good size, producing 40 petals each. They are also carried in clusters of between six and ten blooms per stem. The colour is exquisite – a rich crimson red with tinges of purple. As the flowers mature, they turn a little darker, adding a faint black sheen to the petals which enhances its luxurious effect. The fragrance is strong and intense, having sweet and 'clovey' notes. 'Empereur du Maroc' makes a thorny, compact bush and needs the best feeding for good results. If the flowers are exposed to excessive sunshine, they may burn, resulting in brown petals. In very warm spells, I often lightly cover the plant with a piece of horticultural fleece to give added protection from the bright sunlight. Good air circulation is very important for this rose, as it can be prone to mildew.

A rose I remember from my childhood, especially for its wonderful scent, is 'Fragrant Cloud'. This special rose has won numerous awards since its introduction in the 1960s. The double blooms are of a coral red colour and the flowers are extremely fragrant. 'Fragrant Cloud' is generally quick to repeat flower and, with good feeding and care, is healthy. For best impact and to enjoy the scent, I planted three plants close to the path. The scent is sweet and, on a still summer's evening, can be carried on the air.

'Irish Fire Flame'

'Wild Edric'

'Pierre de Ronsard'

'Shakespeare 2000'

I have been asked what rose I would take to a desert island and several immediately come to mind. Of these, one stands out and that is 'Zéphirine Drouhin'. At Clondeglass, instead of letting them climb, I have planted a row of them and keep them free-standing as a small hedge close to the central path in the garden – a place where I can fully enjoy their beauty along with their wonderful fragrance. This way, the plants also get full air circulation, which helps their health. It is a Bourbon rose, and the scent is penetrating, with strong notes of crushed raspberries and fruit. The colour is bright cerise pink. The blooms are medium sized and of loose formation. A special and remarkable feature of this rose is the fact that it carries no thorns, making it very suitable as a climbing rose in busy areas of the garden, where people may brush it. This rose was raised in France in 1868 and it has stood the test of time. It repeat flowers well throughout the summer and is always a joy to cut and bring indoors.

A red rose I treasure at Clondeglass is David Austin's masterpiece, 'Shakespeare 2000'. The colour is of the richest velvet crimson, which gradually matures to deeper purple tones. The fragrance is rich and full and has the warmth you will find in old-fashioned roses. It is another fantastic flower to use for cutting. Fill a bowl with stems and you will be able to fully appreciate the strong old-world fragrance, which is exquisite and perfectly matches the colours and tones. In good soil, it grows 1m x 0.8m (3.5ft x 2.5ft).

In Clondeglass, one area in particular has been dedicated to growing a wide range of roses. I created this after returning from a trip with Irish gardeners around private gardens of the Netherlands. There, I

admired the rose 'Bonica' and subsequently planted it in Clondeglass in three large groups. This beautiful pink rose helps to create continuity through the rose borders and performs extremely well each summer, providing a bushy plant with plenty of flowers. This also made me look at what other plantings were used in association with roses. I edged two large borders with *Nepeta* 'Six Hills Giant'. This creates a spectacular display with a lavender-like effect. It continues right through the summer and into autumn. I have also added foxgloves and have a particular fondness for the *Digitalis Purpurea* 'Pam's Choice'. This produces large flowers of white with red splashes. For an early display in gaps between roses, I plant aquilegias. They add valuable early colour, which is much needed before the roses begin to flower. These are then followed by low-growing perennial geraniums. For best value, I use *G.* 'Rozeanne'. This has wonderful blue flowers with white centres and makes a very striking groundcover combination. I have found that, by introducing all these plants in and around my roses, I have dramatically increased the insect life in this part of the garden. Bees and butterflies give much enjoyment, as do the hummingbird hawk moths who use the path between the roses as a runway as they take their fill of nectar from the catmint. Here and there throughout the rose border I sprinkle seed of night-scented stock, which adds a heavenly fragrance on warm summer evenings.

Facing the East border, a beautiful rambling rose called 'Veilchenblau', which is a particularly unusual colour and has a wonderful scent.

Oriental Poppies *(Papaver orientale)*

If any plant deserves the title of 'diva' in my border, it has to be *Papaver orientale*. When in full flower, it takes centre stage, usually making a show for around three weeks from the end of June into early July. The display catapults the garden into high summer each year. The flowers can be carried on stems anywhere between 60–90cm (2–3ft) high, and to look inside a newly opening flower is always a special treat. Inside, you'll see a black/purple splashing, which runs outwards on each petal. The powdery stamens have a mascara quality that adds to the beauty. It's like the finest makeup artist has been at work preparing the star for centre stage. Like all theatre, you'll need another plant standing in the wings to take over when these beauties have finished their show.

Above 'Patty's Plum'

Left 'Princess Victoria Louise'

Depending on weather conditions, I sometimes use a discreet support. Rain usually runs off the flowers and, unless very heavy, it generally causes no serious damage. My oriental poppies are amongst the most spectacular perennials I grow. The range of colours is divine and they flower in both double and single forms. The petals have a satiny texture and when fully open they almost look as if they had been made from crêpe paper.

'Patty's Plum' is deservedly popular. The large blooms extend 15cm (6in) across. The colour is straight from an artist's palette – mauve and dusky lavender with velvet-black and purple blotches in the centre. This has become one of my favourites. Last year, I added a newer form of this poppy from Hayloft Plants called 'Ruffled Patty', with equally splendid blooms. Each petal is frilled and ruffled, which creates an even more voluptuous flower. The overall effect adds a bit more pizzazz. These poppies grown together associate very well with *Sanguisorba menziesii*. It's the shape of the flowers that works so well. The elongated plum-coloured flowers contrast beautifully.

Planted in my new border is a very beautiful variety called *P. o.* 'Princess Victoria Louise', which has enormous salmon-pink blossoms, the centre of which have bold black blotches. The darkness of the blotch against the softness of the salmon pink lends depth to the flower and as they open they shimmer. On the other side of the garden I grow Goliath Group 'Beauty of Livermere'. The colour is vivid blood red and contrasts strongly with its deep black centre. This poppy is flamboyant, opulent and outrageous – not a flower for the fainthearted. I always make sure there are other plants like *Dahlia* 'Bishop of Llandaff', with its scarlet flowers and bronze foliage, on hand to fill the gap after this spectacular poppy has finished, to continue the colour display through summer into autumn.

Papaver orientale is easy to grow once you follow a few simple rules. Firstly, it needs perfect drainage, as it produces large, deep roots. Secondly, never let the plant get too wet or too dry, as that will impact on its performance. Thirdly, it is happy to grow in sun or part shade. These poppies are long-lived and can be readily propagated from root cuttings, which are taken

in early spring or autumn. The usual height and spread is around 90cm (3ft) but newer varieties are coming on stream which are more compact and longer flowering. My plants usually flower in late June, so having longer-flowering varieties would be most welcome. There is a wonderful old fully double red form growing at Clondeglass close to the old house. I know this was planted a very, very long time ago and it's not impossible to imagine it growing there 100 years ago. It is testimony to their long life.

A perennial plant that is good to grow around *P. orientalis* to fill the gap after they finish is *Gypsophila*. The pale pink form, 'Flamingo', or the great stalwart double white, 'Bristol Fairy', are the ones to look out for. *Penstemon* also offers superb value and a good range of colours. I also use annuals like cosmos in various shades of pink, and *Nicotiana*. I always try to get the scented form of *Nicotiana* for evening fragrance. After flowering, I tidy up the plants, which helps to prevent disease or other problems. It also makes room for neighbouring plants to fill in. The poppies, being totally hardy, don't seem to mind this.

'Patty's Plum'

Dahlias

Above 'Sam Hopkins'

Right 'Ellen Huston'

For sheer drama in the garden, grow dahlias each year. They provide a long-lasting display and add colour and interest to the borders from summer into autumn. With a little work, the rewards are great.

The dahlias at Clondeglass are planted as pot-grown plants, raised mostly from tubers purchased in April, potted up and then put into the polytunnel where they are carefully watered and gently brought into growth. Small plants from one of the main dahlia specialists in the UK are also added to the garden. These usually arrive in growth around the end of May or beginning of June and will go into the garden only when all signs of frost are over. For best results, the soil is well dug in advance with plenty of compost and organic fertiliser added. This work usually commences several months ahead to allow it all to settle before the planting starts.

Dahlias are divided into many different flowering groups. This helps to make it easier to select the shape of flower you like. At Clondeglass, three different types are usually selected: decorative, semi-cactus, and pompom. All are very different in shape. The colours are varied with reds, purples, mauves and pinks, many in brilliant and rich shades, and they always make a big impact in the borders. New varieties are introduced to grow alongside old stalwarts like 'Arabian Night'. This is a dark, black-red double with medium-sized flowers. I saw a particularly impressive planting of this in June Blake's garden in Wicklow near Dublin, and I found it inspiring. This dahlia stands out very effectively when planted against lighter-coloured foliage plants. Another wonderful dahlia at Clondeglass is 'Moor Palace'. The flowers are pompom in shape and are flamboyant maroon-purple in colour. It also makes a good cut flower.

The late Christopher Lloyd grew dahlias at his famous garden, Great Dixter. He often incorporated them into plantings in this exotic garden and that is where I saw 'Hillcrest Royal' in full flower. It is a magnificent cactus dahlia, which produces blooms of brilliant magenta-purple. The large double flowers have pointed petals and create a show-stopping effect.

Each year at Clondeglass I also grow one of the great dahlia classics, 'Bishop of Llandaff'. This dahlia is known for its magnificent bronze foliage and single bright red flowers. The combination of flowers and leaves sets this dahlia apart from others. It's wonderful when combined with other plants. I try it with different plant combinations and find it's especially effective when used with purples and blues, such as *Verbena bonariensis*, and low-growing geraniums like *G.* 'Rozanne'. It grows 1m in height and is best planted in a group.

When planting out dahlias, it's a good idea to pinch out the growing tips, as this encourages the plants to bush out and to create more flowers.

Slugs and snails are a big problem at Clondeglass and I am aware that young dahlias are particularly attractive to them. A light scattering of organic slug pellets around each plant is most effective. Depending on the weather, this will need to be repeated every week to ten days. Deadheading the plants will help to save energy and will encourage new buds to develop.

Sometimes, the odd earwig is found in flowers and I use my grandmother's method to deal with this. A bamboo cane is inserted among the plants and on the top of the cane is placed an old, smallish terracotta pot stuffed with straw. The pot is placed upside down on the cane. The next morning, earwigs will have retreated into these pots and are easily removed and disposed of.

For best results, dahlias are best positioned in full sun, preferably in a spot sheltered from wind. During their growing season, about every two weeks, give them an organic liquid tomato feed, but be careful not to overdo the feeding – too much can promote soft growth and leave them more prone to greenfly attack.

Species Dahlias

Recently, I saw some species dahlias in Italy and I have taken a special interest in growing some at Clondeglass. As an experiment I started with a few different types in large containers. *D. tenuicaulis* has attractive single pink flowers and reaches a great height of 3–3.5m (10–12ft). The stems are strong and the flowers are produced continuously over many months. Like many species dahlias, it originates in Mexico. This one comes from the mountain forests where the temperature is cooler. However, it does require a sheltered, frost-free position so, come autumn, it will be moved into the polytunnel. There it will be given extra protection and allowed to go on the dry side over the winter months. It requires plenty of water while in growth.

The most unusual of the species dahlias grown at Clondeglass is *D. campanulata*. This is an exceptionally tall-growing plant and, late in summer, it produces hanging flowers, which can be approximately 7cm (3in) in length. The colour is pale pink to white with a deep maroon centre and yellow stamens. From a distance, this dahlia looks quite magnificent as the individual

'Kenora Sunset'

'Western Folly'

flowers give the impression of small handkerchiefs. If grown in a greenhouse, it is attractive to whitefly and needs to be sprayed with an organic insecticide.

Of the three dahlia species I grow, *D. merckii* is probably the easiest and the hardiest. It produces fine foliage and makes mounds of growth approximately 1.2 m (4ft) high. At the height of summer, it's covered in attractive mauve-pink single flowers. Each flower is small and it's the quantity that makes the show.

These species dahlias are best propagated by cuttings. I do these in mid-summer, to allow them to develop a small tuber before winter. They all benefit from an occasional foliar feed. There are different foliar feeds available and I prefer to use organic types. Also, the addition of seaweed in liquid feeds is excellent for stimulating growth and helping to build plants up. The taller types benefit from regular feeding and require

sheltered positions, as wind can cause severe damage. Having a few strong bamboo canes to hand is a good idea. As the stems are not hard, they can easily be cut with something thin like wire, so a soft tie, ideally something strong that is padded with a spongy covering, is perfect for tying the stems to the bamboo canes.

The best position for the taller species is at the back of the border, where it's usually a little more sheltered. I have selected a spot close to the extra large-growing form of *Lobelia tupa*. The position is sunny and sheltered. These plants are not planted out until all signs of frost are gone, though to give them a head start I get them going under glass in pots.

'Kenora Macop'

A dahlia hybrid.

Crocosmias *(Crocosmia)*

Travelling through the Irish countryside, particularly Donegal in the north or Co. Kerry in the south, in mid to late-summer, you will see the roadsides laden with naturalised crocosmias, locally known as montbretia. These exquisite stalwarts create an orange display which adds to the breathtaking scenery.

Above 'Firebird'

Right 'Lucifer'

Overleaf Left, the yellow, very vigorous and strong growing 'George Davison'. Right, 'Solftare', which has distinctive, smoky, pale bronze leaves.

I have always loved crocosmias and have grown them for as long as I can remember. They are an important plant in Clondeglass and add an extra touch of fire and vitality to the borders.

The word 'crocosmia' means 'crocus-scented', so called after the scent of saffron, the pollen of *Crocus sativus*. The first crocosmia to be planted at Clondeglass was *C.* 'Lucifer', in the West border. This is a showy hybrid raised in 1969. It grows 1.2m (4ft) high. The flowers are a rich, vibrant red – very eyecatching. I purposely planted it in drifts on each side of the border to help to link the display. When in full flower, this creates a vibrant and dramatic effect, and adds important unity. For extra impact, it is underplanted with the bold dark purple foliage of *Angelica sylvestris* 'Vicar's Mead' and – for added sparkle – *Verbena bonariensis.*

Further up the border is an old favourite – *C. × crosmiiflora* 'Solfatare'. This is a very attractive old variety with smoky pale bronze foliage, which sets off the apricot yellow flowers – a remarkable combination. The plant grows 65cm (26in) high and received an RHS Award of Garden Merit (AGM) in 1993. It was introduced from France in 1886.

Another special crocosmia that I have grown for many years, and am now happy to have at Clondeglass, is *C. × c.* 'His Majesty'. I first grew this variety at least 25 years ago. I remember planting it in a spot in sunshine

where I'd had a large pile of rotting compost. As a result, the soil was very enriched. The plant loved this spot and responded with a magnificent display. I fell head over heels in love with it and have grown it ever since. It is a large-flowering cultivar which produces an abundant display. The colour is a vivid scarlet-crimson with yellow shades. The centre of each flower is a clear yellow and the combination is striking. This variety has been around since the early 1900s and has received many awards from the RHS.

We all know the expression of being in the right place at the right time. One summer afternoon, I was visiting Helen Dillon's garden in Dublin as she was doing a major job on her front garden. In the centre was a large golden-variegated holly and in front of this grew a fabulous clump of *C.* 'Firebird'. I admired it and was generously offered a piece (which I accepted!). I planted it when I returned home, giving it the best spot and soil I had available. The plant thrived but was extremely slow growing and, though it flowered every year, it took a long time to build up. I have only recently moved it to Clondeglass, where it is planted close to some very vivid blue agapanthus for contrast. *C.* 'Firebird' was raised in 1970 by Blooms Nursery, UK. It grows 75cm (30in) tall, with large flowers of glowing orange-red. This is one of my most treasured plants and is always greatly admired when in full flower.

Also in the collection of crocosmias at Clondeglass is another favourite, 'Emily McKenzie'. This beauty was raised in 1951 in Northumberland, and is noted for its exceptionally large flowers, which are 6–7cm (2.5in) across and are a deep shade of orange with a central blotch of crimson, set off by a paler eye – a stunning combination. It grows around 75cm (30in) high and in full flower it's breathtaking. This is a crocosmia that always draws attention. Large-flowering crocosmias have a reputation for being a little more on the tender side, so I always make a point of covering them with a thick mulch of leaves and a little compost in winter.

Introduced by the late, great plantsman Graham Stuart Thomas, is one of the largest-flowering varieties of all, called *C. × c.* 'Star of the East'. The colour can only be described as a luminescent orange and each individual flower can measure 7cm (2.5in) across. To get the best result, I find 'Star of the East' needs a rich soil and even moisture through the summer. It looks particularly well when planted in association with bold-leaved perennials like hostas. It can be a little bit more difficult to find, but it is worth the effort.

Just planted in the East border at Clondeglass is a group of what is regarded as one of the most distinctive hybrids – *C. × c.* 'Nimbus'. This showy variety was raised in 1918. The large glowing orange flowers have a striking ring of soft brick red. This central ring puts this crocosmia in a league of its own. I await its first flowering at Clondeglass with great anticipation.

Another special crocosmia noted for a central ring in the flower is *C. × c.* 'Prometheus'. The flowers are big and impressive, reaching 9cm (3.5in) across.

The colour is a deep, glowing orange with a central ring of rich red. Raised in 1904, this now rare variety is still grown by collectors and definitely requires some winter protection. It is a greedy plant and enjoys the best organic compost you can provide.

Natives of South Africa, these plants often grow near – but not in – running water. When growing these plants, I provide well-dug soil with plenty of organic matter like very well-rotted manure. Perhaps unsurprisingly, the large-flowered types are the greediest, and benefit from a sprinkle of organic fertiliser at least once a year. I try to avoid using chemical fertilisers as I feel the plants respond better and the soil also appreciates the organic feeding. Sometimes hard to please, crocosmias hate cold and wet soil, and also dislike the opposite – hot and dry. When preparing for their arrival in your garden, treat them as you would any diva, and always provide them with an à la carte menu of the best organic materials you have available.

When planting the corms, I usually plant them 8–10cm (3–4in) deep. This can be done in autumn and they are best covered with a thick layer of fallen leaves for added protection. With a little effort and work on the soil, I find crocosmias very rewarding. Their late-summer display and their vibrant show always take centre stage.

'Lucifer'

Left 'Firebird'

Overleaf The gravel in the path is sandstone, which, when weathered, will match the colour of the walls. In the foreground, on the left, is a geum. Behind, planted in a terracotta pot, is an ornamental banana. Further along is an ornamental grass. At the end of the path can just be seen one of the yews being trained into a double globe.

Autumn & Winter

Autumn and winter are times for planning ahead. The work that goes into the garden now will pay off next year. The planting of bulbs, such as snowdrops, tulips, daffodils and other spring-flowering bulbs, is best carried out in the autumn and early-winter period, usually before the ground becomes too difficult to work or dig. It's also a marvellous time to stand back and take a look at where plants are already doing well and consider how you can complement or enhance existing successful plant combinations. Often a little work can be done on paper before going into the garden to help you decide exactly what goes where.

Rose hips of the *Rosa canina* on a frosty morning.

Witch Hazel *(Hamamelis)*

Right Hamamelis mollis

Of the many winter-flowering shrubs I grow, witch hazel is one of the most remarkable. Without foliage, it's covered from top to bottom in bunches of small, narrow petals. These are sweetly scented and look spectacular against a backdrop of snow.

The main form I grow is *Hamamelis mollis*, which produces pale yellow, ribbon-shaped flowers. A small piece cut and brought indoors will fill the room with its scent. Apart from the beautiful yellow varieties, there are also varieties with orange-coloured flowers. One of the best is *Hamamelis* x *intermedia* 'Jelena'. This also has a marvellous winter fragrance.

The planting position should be carefully thought out beforehand so you get the full benefit of your witch hazel's beauty during the winter months when its foliage has been lost. When planting, prepare the soil in advance, remembering that your witch hazel will last in the same spot for many years to come. The little work you put in now will pay off for many years. Put in plenty of organic matter, which will help the shrub to establish. Also add a dressing of well-rotted compost or manure in spring. Position the plant where it will not get blasted by cold wind – a sheltered spot is best. The protection of an existing hedge or other shrubs is usually all that's needed to get your witch hazel off to a good start.

Witch hazel looks good when underplanted with groups of small bulbs like snowdrops, crocus and aconitum.

Hamamelis x *intermedia* 'Jelena'

Snowdrops *(Galanthus)*

Distinct and beautiful, snowdrops are peerless among early-flowering garden bulbs and are probably among the best loved. I planted snowdrops at Clondeglass for many reasons, but primarily to carry me through the bleakness of winter. It is their simplicity and exquisite beauty that draws me to this harbinger of the new year.

In the last decade, Galanthomania has really caught on, with people collecting and swapping unusual snowdrop varieties. Here in Ireland, we have many notable gardens with good collections of named varieties of snowdrops. One garden in particular is Altamont, near Tullow in Co. Carlow. It and another good garden, Bellefield in Co. Offaly, hold special snowdrop events. These events attract collectors from all over for the opportunity to purchase and swap many of the exceptional rare snowdrops that are now in circulation. I caught this bug many years ago.

One of the first snowdrops I grew was an exceptionally beautiful variety called *G. nivalis* f. *pleniforus* 'Lady Elphinstone'. A double-flowered form, it has yellow markings. It's a very old variety and forms a large clump. My own cherished plant had reached a good size, producing around 15 flowers of the most exquisite pale yellow double bells when, suddenly, the plant collapsed and died just before I had the opportunity to lift and divide it. Luckily, the year before, I had lifted a piece to give it to snowdrop enthusiast Angela Jupe of Bellefield, where it has thrived. On a recent visit, I was offered a piece back. It proves that if you give a plant away and then lose it, there's always a chance of it coming back to you.

On a recent trip to Bellefield to see Angela's collection of over 100 different named varieties, I discovered that I had one in my own small collection that Angela was not growing – *G. plicatus* 'Wendy's Gold'. I was pleased to be able to offer her a bulb to try. This is a very fine yellow-marked snowdrop, which I have found to be slow to clump up. 'Wendy's Gold' is noted as being one of the very best of the yellow snowdrops. The flowers have golden ovaries and the inner segment has the largest yellow markings of any snowdrop. My clump, which I have now moved to Clondeglass, has around 20 bulbs. I saw this variety recently in a well-known UK snowdrop nursery priced at £14 sterling per bulb, so one bulb can turn into an investment if looked after. The yellow colouring can vary a little while it settles in after transplanting.

An Irish snowdrop I recently received is named after the great Irish plantsman David Shackleton. I had been lucky to visit him on many occasions at his amazing walled garden at Beech Park, Clonsilla, Co. Dublin. He was a brilliant plantsman who had a reputation for not tolerating fools gladly. His walled garden contained one of the finest private plant collections in these isles. It was an honour to have been in his company on many occasions. This choice snowdrop is a strong-growing plant which flowers a little later than many others. The flowers are of a good size and the purest white with attractive olive green markings and ovaries. It is a form of *G. elwesii*. I am delighted to have this snowdrop growing in Clondeglass as a memory of this great man.

Another Irish snowdrop I grow is the lovely double *G.* 'Hill Poe'. It is always a great favourite among those who grow it. David Shackleton saved this snowdrop from obscurity by sending a bulb in 1960 to the then famous Giant Snowdrop Company. It was discovered around 1911, growing under a walnut tree in Co. Tipperary, and was first offered for sale nearly 50 years ago. The double flowers are beautifully formed and make a neat, near-perfect rosette. It usually has six outer petals, giving a very pleasing overall effect. This magnificent double remains one of my favourites and I carefully treasure it at Clondeglass.

There are close to 20 different named Irish snowdrops. Many of these are coveted and very desirable. I am lucky to have a small collection at Clondeglass, which I have built up over several years and with the generosity of Irish growers such as Angela Jupe and

Robert Miller. This is a marvellous list, many of which I will enjoy seeking out to plant in Clondeglass, and it includes 'Lady Moore', 'Lady Ainsworth', 'Irish Green', 'Emerald Isle', 'The O'Mahony', 'Kilkenny Giant', 'Kildare', 'Cicely Hall', 'Rowallane' and 'Robin Hall'.

Angela Jupe gave me a plant named after her mother, May Jupe. She discovered this in 1997 in Forthfield Gardens, Palmerstown Road, Dublin. It is a strong grower, with pure white, large flowers with pointed petals. The inner markings have a green inverted 'V' shape with a green blotch above. This choice snowdrop, which colonises well, thrives in heavy soil.

Recently, I planted at Clondeglass some bulbs of the Irish snowdrop 'Straffan'. I received this one from Robert Miller. A very attractive snowdrop, it was originally grown at Straffan House in Co. Kildare. It

'Hill Poe'

G. plicatus 'Wendy's Gold'

is a late-flowering variety with pure white, perfectly formed flowers. The inner markings form a Chinese bridge shape. When this snowdrop settles into its position, it will often reward with a second flowering, extending the season. This adds greatly to its value.

A new Irish snowdrop that's rated very highly is *G. elwesii* 'Barnhill'. This was discovered around the year 2000 by Eimear Gallagher in the garden at Beech Park, Clonsilla, Co. Dublin, the garden originally owned by David Shackleton. The flowers are large and pure white with spear-shaped petals. The ovaries are olive green and the inner markings are a mid green colour with the shape of an inverted 'V'. Above this is a good rich marking of green. This snowdrop is a good grower and promises to have a good future.

Despite growing many of these rare and very desirable snowdrops, I still find the ordinary *G. nivalis* supremely beautiful. I have been lucky to find snowdrops easy to grow at Clondeglass. They seem to like the soil within the walled garden.

I try not to disturb them unless absolutely essential, for instance when they have become overcrowded and division is needed. When selecting a position for planting snowdrops, it's best to choose a site with free-draining soil. If there are any doubts, dig in grit to enhance the drainage. I give my snowdrops a light dressing of organic fertiliser annually. When using fertilisers, I prefer organic feeds, avoiding chemicals, as I use the principal of feeding the soil as well as the plant. I have found the use of EM (see page 158) in liquid form very helpful in establishing bulbs. They usually

'Flore Pleno'   'Kildare'

settle in quite quickly. Also, I never cut or damage the foliage, always allowing it to die back naturally, to build up strength for the following year.

There is great excitement in hunting down, finding and locating snowdrops to add to one's collection by going to plant fairs, specialist garden sales and nurseries. The *RHS Plant Finder* is of great assistance, especially for sourcing particular snowdrops.

Nerines *(Nerine)*

In the early 1990s, I went on a trip with my father to look for interesting plants that were not available in Ireland at the time. On my travels, I visited many nurseries and returned home with the car bulging with plants.

I came across some exciting old Irish cultivars of *Nerine sarniensis*. Raised in the late 1950s and early 1960s by Miss Doris Findlater, the varieties I returned with included some of her finest, including the brilliant red 'Glensavage Gem', 'Tweedledee' and 'Tweedledum' (named after Lewis Carroll's famous fantasy characters), 'The Giraffe' and 'The Spider'. These are just a few of the results of Miss Findlater's hybridising work. Many of her named varieties have now been lost, so it was a great pleasure for me to return home to Ireland with these special plants.

I had a bespoke glasshouse built at Clondeglass with the help of Irish craftsmen for my collection. Although nerines can be shy to flower, the display is often breathtaking. The flowers have a jewel-like quality and some varieties even have a sparkle on their petals. I expanded my collection from bulbs that I purchased from Nicholas de Rothschild at Exbury in Southampton. Exbury Gardens is famous for its rhododendrons and azaleas, but Nicholas has also created one of the finest private collections of nerines to be found anywhere. The great plantsman Sir Peter Smithers, who lived in Vico Morcote in Switzerland, had spent the 1970s and 1980s hybridising and improving nerines he had originally obtained from Exbury. In 1995, Sir Peter decided that the collection he had developed should return to Exbury. Today, those Exbury/Vico nerines contribute to the outstanding hybrids coming from Nicholas de Rothschild's own work.

It's interesting to note from Charles Nelson's work that the National Botanic Gardens in Glasnevin, Dublin, had run a nerine-breeding programme where in excess of 100 cultivars were named. Sadly, the entire collection was wiped out on a frosty night in the 1930s. In the splendid book *An Irish Florilegium: Vol II*, there are fine watercolour paintings of Miss Findlater's nerines by one of Ireland's greatest botanical artists, Wendy Walsh, including a portrait of *N.* 'Glensavage Gem'.

Nerines originate from South Africa, where there are around 30 species. Greek mythology suggests that the name *Nerine* came from Nereide, the daughter of Nereus, son of Oceanus. The genus name was given in 1820 by the Reverend William Herbert. Nerines were extremely popular in Guernsey, where they were known as the Guernsey lily. It is interesting to note that the Romans called the island Sarnia, probably leading to the species name '*sarniensis*'. The nerine hybrids that are available from specialist nurseries today are based on *N. sarniensis*. They are easy to cultivate, and require perfect drainage and good-quality compost. I grow my most precious plants in terracotta pots with added grit.

For additional protection in winter, I cover the interior of my wooden greenhouse with plastic bubble wrap. This is easy to put up using drawing pins. Nerines have no tolerance for frost, but are happy in cool winter conditions that don't drop below 3°C.

Flowering usually commences in October. It's important to allow flowering stems to naturally die back on the plant, so that all possible energy goes back into the bulb. The same applies to foliage. When they start into their dormant period, the leaves will turn yellow and eventually die. Don't remove them until they are completely withered and dry. While in growth, nerines appreciate a fortnightly weak liquid organic tomato feed, especially when established. By doing this, you can make an enormous difference to the quantity of flowers you receive. Never leave nerines standing in water, and, when repotting, add horticultural grit to soil-based compost. I like to use old crocks in the bottom of the pot for extra drainage. If a terracotta pot is accidentally broken, I always put the pieces to one side until I need them for jobs like this.

Correct watering is the key to maintaining nerines. Ideally, they should be given their last watering at the end of July. About a week to a fortnight after that, if you feel it necessary, you can give them a last soaking to make sure that all roots are hydrated before they go into their long dormant period.

Some of the best specialist nurseries are in the UK and it's worthwhile checking out the *RHS Plant Finder*, which carries a wide range of named cultivars. Because of modern hybridising and the work of people like Nicholas de Rothschild and Sir Peter Smithers, among others, there is an array of colours and types to choose from. Every shade of pink, scarlet, plum and purple is available, and two-toned varieties can be found.

During a period of illness, my nerines were neglected. Fortunately, I did not lose many plants, but it was at a crucial time when they needed to be fed and watered. This had a big impact on the collection, as I lost a season of flowers. Thankfully, the important Irish cultivars survived along with many other hybrids. I look forward to autumn, when I expect a great display, and I plan on adding more to the collection over time.

Left A mixture of hybrid *Nerine sarniensis*, grown in the nerine house. Clockwise, from top left: 'Natasha', 'Uganda', 'Dame Alice', 'Menelaus', 'Strawberry Parfait', 'Brighton Rock', 'Amschel'.

'Fleeting Dream'

'Strawberry Parfait'

'Natasha'

'Dame Alice'

Hellebores *(Helleborus)*

Above and right
Ashwood Nursery Double

This is a large group of plants with over 20 different species. When I first started to work on the gardens at Clondeglass, hellebores were extremely popular. Over many years, that popularity has increased further, making them one of the most sought-after of early-flowering plants.

The range of colours available today is wonderful, but it's not just the colours that appeal. A wide range of shapes, from anemone-shaped through to fully double blooms, are now available. The hybrids, which have been developed from *H. orientalis*, give a great winter display. Each year, I add a few new types to the garden. These are usually from Ashwood Nurseries, who are the leaders in hellebore hybridising. Each year at Clondeglass, between January and February, and even up to the end of March, hellebores are in flower. They are a favourite and never fail to captivate my attention when they come into bloom. One plant that stands out is an unnamed double-flowered hybrid, which is white splashed with burgundy red. Providing your soil is not too dry or damp, hellebores will be happy, as they resent extremes. A well-dug soil with plenty of organic garden compost or well-rotted manure will give them exactly what they need. With older plants, I annually mulch them with some very well-rotted compost. Through the summer, an occasional liquid feed is given, especially to the younger plants.

When a clump gets too big, usually after many years of growth in one spot, it is time to divide. This will help to rejuvenate the clump and give a fresh start to the plants. Newly divided plants may take a year or two to settle in, but once re-established they will come back into full force. Hellebores can also be started from seed and, each year, I collect a few seeds from existing plants and sow them, gently transplanting them on to a spot where they have plenty of room to develop, allowing them to form their first flowers. Occasionally, I will buy seed from a reputable source to add extra vigour and vitality to the collection. It's great fun selecting and picking something new each year.

'Pretty Ellen Red'

'White Spotted Lady'

'Pretty Ellen Pink'

'Pink Spotted Lady'

Daffodils *Narcissus*

At Clondeglass, I enjoy growing many different types of daffodil and narcissus. Over the last ten years, several new varieties have been added and the garden now boasts close to 60 different types. They are always planted with one important thing in mind: to create as long a flowering season as possible. The daffodils are purchased in late summer or early autumn and planted in groups in selected spots. By choosing different varieties and different styles of flower, it's possible to have them in bloom from January until the end of May.

The first daffodil to flower at Clondeglass – sometimes as early as the end of December, but certainly by January – is a yellow variety with a typical trumpet shape, known as 'Rijnveld's Early Sensation'. I always make sure it's planted in a sheltered spot where the early flowers won't be damaged by strong wind. I try to add a few extra each year to help provide cut flowers for the house. They're always a great joy, especially when they're brought indoors.

Another early flowering daffodil grown at Clondeglass is the narcissus 'Rip Van Winkle'. This unusual short double-flowered daffodil is an Irish cultivar that was raised in Co. Cork in 1884. The flowers usually appear between February and March and don't grow more than 20cm (8in) in height. The petals have a greenish yellow tinge when in full flower. Fully open, it looks different to every other daffodil and always draws attention. Plant approximately 10–12cm (4–5in) deep and leave a gap between each bulb, especially if putting in a group of ten or more. This daffodil enjoys a position in full sun but will grow equally well in part shade. The key is to make sure that the soil is free-draining and planting should be carried out in late summer or early autumn. This small daffodil associates well with spring-flowering plants and can make a very strong impact when grouped in clumps and spaced throughout a border.

'Rijnveld's Early Sensation'

FABULOUS
Foliage

Clondeglass

Purple-leaved Plants

I have always appreciated plants whose main impact is their foliage. It's difficult to find a plant that adds as much drama to the garden as one with purple leaves. If carefully positioned and planned, it can add an extra dimension to your planting schemes, as well as a subtle but powerful statement that is rarely obtained from a flowering plant.

What follows is a selection of just a few of my favourite purple foliage plants. There is a wide range to choose from and a trip to a local garden centre or nursery will reveal many plants that can be used to great effect in your borders.

Previous Schefflera macrophylla BSWJ9788, which was collected in North Vietnam by Bleddyn and Sue Wynn-Jones of Crûg Farm Plants, and which they describe as the most hardy introduction of this genus that they have ever made.

Left Fuchsia excorticata 'Purpurea'

Above Brachyglottis repanda 'Purpurea'

Right Flowering Fuschia excorticata 'Purpurea'.

Fuchsia excorticata 'Purpurea'

Over 20 years ago, the great plant collector Carl Dacus gave me a present of an extraordinary fuchsia with purple leaves – *F. excorticata* 'Purpurea'. This delightful plant grew in my parent's front garden until I changed the design to include some raised beds. The fuchsia had to be moved, but it didn't like the idea and it died. I was sorry I hadn't taken cuttings and regretted the loss, as it had been such a striking focal point. Many years later, I came across the same plant growing in Carmel Duignan's garden. This time the plant was in full flower, with each flower carrying stamens with bright blue pollen, adding dramatically to the overall effect. You don't expect to see a fuchsia with rich purple foliage covered in small flowers. Carmel kindly gave me a plant, which I carefully positioned at Clondeglass. I have never seen this purple-leaved form in any other garden. I recall making an enquiry about this plant at the New Zealand exhibition staged at the Chelsea Flower Show several years ago, and being told by a native plant expert that this particular form does appear in a few places in the wild, and is regarded as a New Zealand native. Yet the purple version is uncommon. The foliage is exquisitely beautiful when the plant is caught by sunlight, with each leaf taking on a purplish opalescent quality. It does not grow too large and is a treasured plant at Clondeglass.

Although this particular fuchsia is not widely available, like all fuchsias it's extremely easy to propagate by cuttings. Small 10–12cm (4–5in) cuttings placed around the edge of a pot in free-draining compost covered with a clear plastic bag, with a small amount of rooting hormone, will take 2–3 weeks to develop a root system. Once the root systems have started to develop, they should be potted on into individual 7.5cm (3in)

flower pots, again using frcc-draining compost. Keep evenly moist in a sheltered spot outside. A coldframe would be ideal. Also, a little extra protection against slug or snail damage is advisable at this stage, as new shoots are very soft and vulnerable. It always seems to be a small plant that you're nurturing that gets attacked, but the added protection of a coldframe and some organic slug pellets is a good idea. When you're finally planting out in the garden, this fuschia likes a sunny position sheltered from cold wind, such as at the base of a sheltered, sunny wall.

Brachyglottis repanda 'Purpurea'

This is another of my treasured purple-leaved plants, one that I have also grown over the last 25 years. I recall the late gardener John Conan from Graigueconna telling me about this plant. The reverse side of the leaf is covered in a soft, white felt. The story goes that a Maori tribe used these leaves to write love tokens and letters to ones they admired. I told the story for many years when I showed the plant at talks, until on one occasion I was told by a member of the audience that the Maoris had no written language. Well, that burst that particular bubble. This beautiful plant is tender. I acquired my first plant from Robert Walker of Fernhill Gardens in the foothills of the Dublin mountains. Robert had a small nursery full of interesting plants. He explained that he had propagated it from a plant growing on an island owned by his family off the south-west coast of Ireland. I grew the plant for many years and then came across it at Brian Cross's garden, Lakemount, in Glanmire, Co. Cork, growing in his conservatory. It grew there for many years, until unfortunately it died. Right now, several of us are on the trail to find it again and I already have a spot marked for it at Clondeglass.

Sambucus 'Black Lace'

More readily available, and also with very attractive leaves, is *S.* 'Black Lace'. I planted it in a row under *Laburnum vossii* at the entrance to Clondeglass. It has settled in and makes an impressive display. The foliage is darkest burgundy-black in colour and, as the cultivar name suggests, each leaf is finely dissected like lace. When in flower, it produces the typical white elder-shaped flower tinged with pink. One year, a good friend, Brian O'Donnell, asked if he could take the flowers to make elderflower cordial. He did this and it made the most superb pink-coloured and typically elderflower-flavoured drink.

The plant is easy to grow and appreciates being cut back from time to time. This encourages strong new shoots. I also mulch annually with well-rotted garden compost. There are other purple-leaved forms of *Sambucus* but 'Black Lace' has become my favourite.

ELDERFLOWER CORDIAL RECIPE

Collect about 20 fresh flower heads. I usually use a bucket for this job. Add them to 1 litre (2 pints) of water. Chop up two lemons and add them, along with 50g (2oz) of citric acid and 2kg (4½lb) of sugar. Warm this mix until the sugar has dissolved (don't boil it), and then leave to stand and cool overnight. The next day, strain the cordial into bottles.

Left Sambucus 'Black Lace' grown beneath *Laburnum vossii.*

Sambucus 'Black Lace' showing pale pink flower.

Rheum palmatum 'Atrosanguineum' (Ornamental Rhubarb)

On a trip to Beth Chatto's inspiring gardens in Colchester, Essex, in the 1980s, I came across *Rheum palmatum* 'Atrosanguineum' (which is also known as 'Atropurpureum'), the ornamental rhubarb. Its exceptionally striking shape and colour stuck in my memory, so when I began to choose plants for Clondeglass ornamental rhubarb was high on my list of must-haves. It took a little effort, but I was able to acquire two plants. These were positioned on either side of the West border, in soil prepared using plenty of well-rotted farmyard manure and a dressing of organic chicken pellets, where they continue to grow very happily to this day. New growth emerges in spring. The young leaves are a deep, rosy purple and the dramatic foliage often attracts attention and admiring comments.

Cercis canadensis 'Forest Pansy'

'Forest Pansy' is a superb small tree with attractive purple foliage. The new foliage emerges a bright purple with rich red tones and, as the season progresses, this changes, taking on a deep, dark green tinge. Best planted where it will get full protection from hard winter winds, in Clondeglass it has the shelter of other plants as well as a sunny location. The flowers appear on the bark and are a rich, deep pink colour – most attractive early in the year. The only problem I have had with this plant was an attack of scale insects. Because the plant wasn't large, I was able to deal with this by hand. I was lucky that the tree was still young and I quickly got the problem under control. Before I planted it at Clondeglass, I had grown this particular variety in a large container where it was happy for many years.

It appreciates good-quality soil and free drainage. In one of my borders I have a large swathe of the purple-foliaged *Angelica sylvestris* 'Vicar's Mead'. I positioned this in front of a well-established large grouping of the fiery *Crocosmia* 'Lucifer', which stretches from one side of the border to the other. The purple-leaved angelica is strong-growing, and makes a short-lived perennial which will come again if you let it self-seed. The real beauty comes from the maroon-purple foliage, which is also the same colour as the stems. I'm inclined to treat this plant more as a hardy biennial. Insects love the flowers, and you usually see hoverflies around the plant when in full flower. It appreciates good soil, and when it gets the right growing conditions it can reach 1.5m (5ft) high. The flowers are formed in umbels and have a slight scent of honey.

Left In the foreground, the striking purple foliage of *Rheum palmatum* 'Astrosanguiem'.

C. canadensis 'Forest Pansy '

Vitis vinifera 'Purpurea'

I've always admired the purple-leaved vine. Its ornamental foliage is magnificent when it covers a wall. I planted one last year on the south-west facing corner of Clondeglass, close to the cottage. For support, I'm using a combination of wires and metal hooks in the wall. Vines are greedy feeders, so it's important to get this plant off to the very best start. The ground in this corner contains lots of broken old clay pots, which add to the drainage. I added a lot of extra garden compost and well-rotted manure. My neighbours, the Bennetts, have been very generous with manure from their farm, and this I have rotted and incorporated into the ground in this area. The foliage is the typical vine leaf, except that it is a rich, dark purple colour.

To grow this plant well, it needs careful training. Vines are best pruned in winter. A little pruning can be carried out in summer, but remember that if a vine is cut when in growth it is very vulnerable to bleeding.

This is when sap pours out freely from the cut and the plant will suffer. If in doubt, it's always best to get the help of a professional when it comes to cutting back any vine. You're growing this for its ornamental foliage rather than its grapes. I recommend leaving the fruit for the birds. This deciduous climber is fully hardy and, when happy, it can grow up to at least 9m (30ft) in height.

Acacia baileyana 'Purpurea'

In another spot, I was keen to plant something much larger. I was inspired by a large purple shrub/small tree growing in Carmel Duignan's Dublin garden – *Acacia baileyana* 'Purpurea'. Carmel had grown this stunning foliage plant from seed, and it enjoyed a sheltered spot where it had grown for many years. I was confident that I would be able to grow this exquisite beauty. The foliage is what makes this plant so special. New growth is purple-tinged and appears to have a bloom like you sometimes find on a bunch of purple grapes.

Vitis vinifera 'Purpurea'

Acacia baileyana 'Purpurea'

This colour is highlighted against the steely blue foliage, which develops as the tree matures, creating a contrasting background. In Carmel's garden this was a showstopper for many years, so I carefully positioned a small plant. But in the very bad winter of 2010 I lost it. The plant was too young and didn't survive the intense cold that Clondeglass experienced. This has not put me off, as I'm determined to have another go. I've learned that the plant appreciates good drainage and a sunny spot. A little protection in winter with horticultural fleece should help me to carry it through its early years. All going well, the plant should mature in time and eventually produce yellow mimosa flowers in spring.

Zanthoxylum piperitum 'Purple Leaved'

Nick Macer of Pan-Global Plants recommended a very interesting purple-foliage shrub – *Zanthoxylum piperitum* 'Purple Leaved'. Described as most desired among those who have seen it, this is an extremely rare form of the Japan pepper. The purple foliage is pinnate and aromatic when crushed. The stems are spiny, so positioning is important. I have given my plant the best-quality soil by my east-facing wall. It is still young, but I have great expectations as it develops. During winter months, it is deciduous and I have positioned it near hellebores to create early interest.

Acer palmatum dissectum

One of the most attractive shrubs growing in Clondeglass is a cut-leafed Japanese maple called *Acer palmatum dissectum*; 'palmatum' describes the shape of the leaf, and 'dissectum' indicates that the leaf is finely dissected. This happens to be a purple-leafed form, but it's also available in green. Slow-growing, it doesn't like to dry out, but it's equally important for it not to be too wet. Finding an appropriate sheltered spot is essential for success with this type of maple. Over many years, it will develop a very beautiful shape, and in winter, when all the foliage has fallen, the twisted stems are exposed, and look extremely attractive.

Japanese maples are especially fond of neutral to acidic soil, so digging in plenty of acidic compost when planting will benefit the plant. Also, the hedges in the garden help to provide extra protection, especially for the new growth that unfolds from the plant in spring. I hear of more maples dying within their first few years from wind exposure than any other problem.

When planting a Japanese maple, there are many named varieties available, so if you're lucky enough to have space, seek the advice of an expert from your local garden centre before choosing.

Acer palmatum dissectum (purple form)

Variegated Plants

The range of variegated plants grown today is enormous. All you have to do is to walk around a well-stocked garden centre to get an idea of the numbers available. Over the years, I have found myself growing countless variegated plants, some successfully and others less so. I find myself now being a little more choosy about what variegated plants I grow. There are some plant groups, such as hostas, where variegation is an important part of their character and new types are constantly appearing. Then there are other plant groups, for instance roses, where variegation plays no role and does not seem to add any extra beauty or decorative character.

With careful positioning, variegated plants add light and drama to your garden. Evergreen varieties give extra value in winter, when there is a shortage of colour from flowers. Sometimes variegated plants can be more difficult to grow, needing special attention. Whether you like them or not, it is hard to deny that their value and popularity in modern gardens is increasing.

Rubus fruticosus 'Variegatus'. It needs tender loving care as it doesn't have the vigour of the wild bramble. It likes semi-shade and is best planted in soil that doesn't dry out.

Aralia elata 'Aureovariegata'

Aralia elata 'Variegata'

I first saw *A. elata* 'Variegata' as a spectacular specimen growing in the 1970s at Marlfield Garden Centre in south Co. Dublin, where it had been planted by the much-loved Irish television gardener Barney Johnson. The specimen there had been planted in a sheltered, sunny spot and it developed into a striking plant approximately 2.5m (8ft) high, branching and making a fabulous focal point. The large leaves have an umbrella-like effect. Each leaf opens with a creamy edge, which turns white. The foliage is divided and around 90cm (3ft) long. The multitude of exotic-looking, frond-like leaves gives the full plant an architectural effect. The Royal Horticultural Society had given this plant their prestigious Award of Garden Merit (AGM).

In Clondeglass, I planted two several years ago. They are fully hardy and will tolerate light shade or sunlight. You need to be careful when planting as these variegated forms are grafted (which also makes them expensive to buy). Of the two plants, one of them is the golden-variegated form *Aralia elata* 'Aureovariegata'. The leaves are the same size, the difference being they have a more golden colour instead of the silver. These are deciduous large shrubs or small trees. When planting, it is important to avoid a spot where they would be exposed to strong winds, as this can cause severe damage as the plant matures. An added bonus is the clusters of small white flowers in late summer and early autumn. But do take heed: the stems can be extremely spiny, and they are not suitable where small children will be playing.

Because the plant is grafted, you can occasionally get a green shoot sprouting from the ground underneath the plant. Remove these straight away, making sure to remove the root. Otherwise, energy will go straight into developing green-leaved shoots. They are not difficult to dig out.

I have always loved these aralias and they make the perfect stand-out specimen plant if you have room in your garden. They can also be grown in a large tub or half barrel, provided it is given good drainage and shelter. It's worth trying this if you're limited on space.

Azara macrophylla 'Variegata'

A. macrophylla 'Variegata' comes from South America and grows into a very elegant large shrub. Some people may consider it a small tree. I have always found it to be tender and have tried growing it in different spots on many occasions. Each time I see the plant, something draws me to it and I'm always happy to try it again. Now when planting it, I select a very sheltered wall, ideally in sun and protected from wind. I prepare the soil well in advance of planting. At Clondeglass, I'm

now trying two different forms: *A. m.* 'Variegata' and *A. serrata* 'Aureovariegata'. Both are extremely slow. Their branches make attractive fan shapes and the individual leaves are very small. On *A. m.* 'Variegata' there is a tiny tassel-shaped flower made up of a small cluster of stamens, pale yellow in colour. The flower is not showy but it makes up for this by having a splendid sweet vanilla fragrance, which travels in the air in late winter and early spring. The flowers are so hard to notice, you usually detect the scent first and have to go hunting to find its source. The variegated *A. serrata* can be difficult to establish. The individual small leaves are

a little bit larger than those of *A. macrophylla*, and the golden variegation is very attractive. This one is more difficult to obtain, so I do everything I can to encourage it, but I think it is the hard frost in winter that's the real problem.

Convallaria majalis '**Variegata**'

I grow several variegated forms of lily of the valley *C. majalis* 'Variegata'. I planted this many years ago, and when I bought it, it was called 'Albostriata'. The plant has the typical paddle-shaped leaves of regular lily of the valley, but each leaf is covered in golden stripes.

This choice variety has been in gardens since the 1830s, though it is still scarce. Another variegated variety that established with great ease in my parents' garden is called *C. m.* 'Green Tapestry'. This unusual form has leaves which are mottled and splashed with cream, yellow and pale green, creating a very pleasing effect. I am moving some of this variety to Clondeglass this spring. The flowers on both varieties are exquisitely fragrant, and the short stems with white bells make very good small cut flowers. Just a few are powerful enough to scent a room with their delicious sweet scent. Every part of this plant is poisonous.

Once established, the plant needs plenty of room to spread. It will grow in most well-drained soils and the variegated forms are best planted where they can get a little sun. There are many different cultivars of *C. majalis* grown in gardens. My good friend Carmel Duignan gave me some rhizomes of *C. m.* var. *rosea*, a pale pink form which I have planted beside a yew hedge.

Liriodendron tulipifera 'Aureomarginatum'

There is a very good variegated tulip tree, *L. tulipifera* 'Aureomarginatum', which I grow at the entrance to Clondeglass. The position is bright and sunny and this tree, which is rarely seen in Irish gardens, is proving to be fully hardy and happy in this spot. The variegated leaves are very eye catching in spring and summer. The margins of each leaf are yellow gold. My tree is not mature enough yet to produce the tulip-shaped flowers that give this tree its common name.

In my garden, I am trying many other variegated plants. Along the edge of my border, I recently planted a variegated form of wild blackberry (*Rubus fruticosus*). I had seen it growing many years ago in the famous Wicklow garden at Mount Usher, so when I found a plant I was curious to try it. The foliage is attractive and margined with white edges. It's extremely slow-growing, so time will tell.

*Below Magnolia
grandiflora* 'Clondeglass
Gold'

*Right Ophiopogon
planiscapus* 'Nigrescens
Variegata'

Magnolia grandiflora

The most spectacular variegated plant at Clondeglass is a variegated version of *M. grandiflora*. Two of these plants were given to me many years ago with the story that they had originated from Russia. Each plant is about 1.8m (6ft) high and is very slow-growing. The foliage is large and glossy, with each leaf splashed and marbled with gold. The plants have flowered and produced the typical *M. grandiflora* blooms. Each flower is large and opens white, turning to rich cream. The scent is wonderful. The plants arrived to me with no cultivar name, so one of my family has suggested that I call them 'Clondeglass Gold'.

M. grandiflora enjoys a sunny position and appreciates well-drained soil. To give a little added protection from sharp, cold winds in winter, I cover them with fleece bags. The bags need to be tied in place as, in a windy spell, it is possible for them to be blown off the plant. So, without securing too tightly, I tie these to the base of each tree.

Ophiopogon planiscapus **'Nigrescens Variegata'**

Around the same time I was given the *M. grandiflora*, I was sent another interesting variegated plant called *O. planiscapus* 'Nigrescens Variegata'. The edge of each black leaf has a thin white line. This very fine white line stands out on the darkness of the leaf. I grow this more for its curiosity than great beauty. It sits on the edge of one of my borders, where it grows very, very slowly.

Golden-leaved Plants

Using golden-leaved plants in Clondeglass adds splashes of sunlight throughout the garden. Golden foliage works extremely well when combined with other coloured leaves and stands out against darker backgrounds. When sunlight catches the golden colour, it helps to illuminate it, giving greater richness and depth to a display.

Rhus typhina 'Tiger Eye'

Rhus typhina

In the double border that leads up towards the cottage, I was very keen to include strong visual plants to add a little drama. And I found the perfect plant – *R. typhina* 'Tiger Eye'. I was reluctant to plant it initially, as it has a reputation for spreading and suckering, but I was assured that the variety 'Tiger Eye' would not do this. I can now say, five years on, that it has behaved itself and is still small and neat. It has turned out to be a show stopper. I planted two, one on either side of the border. The foliage is lacy and ferny and the colouring is a brilliant yellow. This is set off by the stems, which have a velvety texture and are salmon orange in colour. The overall appearance is elegant.

I have found it easy to grow and it doesn't seem to be fussy about soil. I used it as a focal point on each side of the border. On the right-hand side, I planted a combination around it that included kale, for its wonderfully shaped leaves and bold, dark colour. In front of the *Rhus* I added a group of variegated agapanthus. Beside this is a sweep of rich yellow *C.* × *crocosmiiflora* 'Mount Usher'. To bring the drama to life, I planted a cerise cactus-flowered dahlia called 'Hillcrest Royal' and, in front of that, a rich pink decorative dahlia called 'Bargaly Blush'. These create a shock and give impact to the display.

On the opposite side of the path, the *R. typhina* 'Tiger Eye' acted as an anchor for the next display I wanted to create. I very much wanted this to be different, so I set about selecting a completely contrasting range with an emphasis on foliage colour and shape. I planted a group of canna – a variety called 'Durban', which has bold, dark-coloured leaves that are brightly striped with

Canna 'Durban'

orange and red. At the very edge of the path, I included a group of brilliant orange Siberian wallflowers. Behind these was planted a good-sized clump of the purple-leaved beet *Beta vulgaris* 'Bull's Blood'. To one side, and just behind the *Rhus*, I planted the vibrant and almost electric-blue *Salvia patens*, and in front of the *Rhus* was a large group of alliums, which I allowed to go to seed. Also in this combination I added a maroon-coloured decorative dahlia and some agapanthus, to give richness to the display.

The beauty of *R. typhina* 'Tiger Eye' is the number of possibilities it creates with each season. In spring, I can add tulips and other spring-flowering plants. In early summer, I could use groups of orange or yellow crown imperials. In flower, they create excitement. Using this plant as an anchor plant for displays in the border, which change with the seasons, adds interest each year. I am limited only by my imagination.

Ribes sanguinem 'Brocklebankii'

Another golden-leaved plant that has only been added to Clondeglass in recent years is the golden-leaved *Ribes sanguineum* 'Brocklebankii'. This beauty really stands out in flower, as the rich pink flowers contrast wonderfully with the golden foliage. In spring, it gives a spectacular display and is always very showy, attracting attention. This ribes is growing on the east-facing part of the garden, where the soil is very well prepared. It's surrounded by spring-flowering plants, including hyacinth, narcissus and many others. Not a particularly fast-growing plant, it remains neat and tidy, requiring very little pruning. After flowering, occasionally the plant sets fruit, which is usually eaten by the birds. This is never a problem, as by this point it has already given a wonderful display.

Philadelphus coronarius 'Aureus'

Not far away is another golden-leaved shrub – *Philadelphus coronarius* 'Aureus'. New growth is bright, rich gold in colour and, as the foliage matures, it becomes a softer yellow. In high summer, the plant is covered in white flowers and the scent is absolutely magnificent, travelling all around the garden from just one plant. Although it is not demanding, it can be a little lax in its growth, requiring occasional tidying, with a light cutting back. I usually do this after flowering.

Overleaf
R. typhina 'Tiger Eye' planted next to a dark-leaved dahlia.

Ribes sanguinem 'Brocklebankii'

Philadelphus coronarius 'Aureus'

GARDENING
Practicalities

Clondeglass

Soil

Your soil is possibly the most important element in your garden. I remember being told many years ago that it is essential to feed your soil rather than give the food directly to the plants. Following this advice at Clondeglass has made an enormous difference, both to the quality of the existing soil and to that of the plants I grow.

Since my serious illness, I find myself looking at things in the garden in a different way. I'm now reluctant to use chemicals and find my gardening practices going in a much more organic direction. When preparing beds and borders, I use a Husqvarna rotovator. Providing stones have been taken out of the way, this does amazing work – often that of three or four people, and in a much shorter time.

I'm lucky at Clondeglass that the general soil quality is good. When I came here, the garden had been neglected for at least 70 years, with only sheep and lambs grazing on it. No strong chemicals or fertilizers had been used. The quality of the soil was probably also down to years of good cultivation in the past. The garden was built in the early 1920s, when hands-on labour was more readily available. Being a traditional walled garden used mostly for productive crops, it probably saw the benefit of regular applications of compost.

The growing and vegetable area.

Drainage

At the very beginning I realised the importance of good drainage. I knew this would impact on not only what I grew in the garden but also on the quality of the soil. With a little investigation, I was able to discover which areas retained moisture better than others and which parts dried out quicker. This was important because, when it came to selecting plants, I was able to choose those that would like those particular conditions. *Euphorbia*, for example, love sun and will tolerate drought. *Iris germanica* like free-draining soil that never gets too wet and will not grow where it is damp.

pH testing

When digging, I discovered that the soil in Clondeglass is deeper in some parts than others, and I take this into account when planting. I only discovered this by digging. Also, there were areas that were much more stony than others, and I was able to retrieve these stones and use them in the base of paths, so nothing went to waste. Early on, I was curious about the pH of my soil, as that would also affect the plants I would grow. I bought a pH testing kit at a local garden centre. This was not expensive and was very easy to use. By taking samples around the garden at various points, as well as samples from below surface level, I was able to map out a rough picture of what my soil pH was like. In most of the garden, it turned out to be neutral, but in other parts, possibly where lime had been used, it was more alkaline. Just outside the wall, where I planted lots of hydrangeas, they revealed the pH by flowering in both pink and blue. Plants closer to the wall were obviously receiving lime from the mortar in the wall and that was turning them pink. Hydrangeas grown a little further away had more neutral to slightly acid conditions and flowered in various shades of blue.

Manure

I have taken in well-rotted manure from my neighbours, the Bennetts, and have further rotted it down before using it. This provided very good conditioning, especially useful when planting. I have also added organic calcified seaweed to some of the borders, with very good effects. I always try to use Irish-made organic products and have recently been using an organic pellet called Seamungus. This is based on a recipe using chicken manure and other organic ingredients. Another product with a high potassium content, ideal for fruit, roses and flowering plants, is Sudden Impact.

EM

I also add diluted EM (Effective Micro-organisms) to my soil. I get this preparation from Natasha Harty of Microbe Solutions, based in Middleton, Co. Cork. As a gardener, it helps if you think of your soil as a living entity. Millions of microbes and micro-organisms live in the soil, along with a huge array of fungal organisms. All of these help to keep the soil healthy.

They often work in conjunction with plant roots and release important nutrients. At Clondeglass, I use EM on a regular basis. Developed in Japan in the 1970s by Professor of Horticulture Dr Teruo Higa, EM is widely used in over 120 countries. It is a liquid culture of natural, non-genetically modified beneficial microbes. I follow the instructions and apply to the soil with my watering can, using a sprinkle bar. I find this a more effective and efficient way of applying it than using a regular rose. It should be noted that it has a limited shelf life, as it is a living product, in the same way as yogurt in your fridge is alive and should be used when active. At Clondeglass, I find EM helpful when I am establishing new plants. It is used more as a tonic than a feed, applied every four to six weeks in areas where the plants would benefit from a boost.

Horse manure

I occasionally supplement my own compost with another Irish-made organic product called Gee-up. This is an odourless horse manure that has been well rotted. It is produced near Bantry in Co. Cork and contains a full range of minor and major nutrients. It also adds humus to your soil and is pH neutral, as is most of the soil in my garden. I use this along with my own compost as a mulch around plants in autumn, to add a little extra protection where needed. It slowly works its way into the soil. I do the same again in spring, when it can be used in drier areas to help to retain moisture. Since it is totally organic, I find it improves the quality of the soil in these areas.

All of this has increased the vitality of my soil and I have noticed that the worm count is up, thus adding another soil-improving constituent.

Compost

At Clondeglass, I make my own compost from a mixture of different materials, both green and (when possible) brown, and it has become one of the most valuable things I use. When fully rotted, it resembles plum pudding mixture. It has no bad smell and is beautiful to use. It does wonders for the soil at Clondeglass, and is doubly satisfying to use because it is a case of recycling – turning a waste material into a beneficial product.

Homemade garden compost is worth its weight in gold, and I am a firm believer that everyone should have at least one compost heap. Caring for your soil is, in my opinion, the key to successful gardening and one of the best ways to do this is to incorporate as much organic matter/compost as possible.

As I mentioned, I think of my garden soil as a living entity, and my compost helps to feed it. Good soil is full of millions of essential micro-organisms, and by adding compost to it you contribute to their health and at the same time improve your soil's drainage and fertility. The roots of the plants you grow will also love it.

When making compost, remember it needs time to mature, as adding fresh compost or manures to your soil can harm it. This is because, as the composting process begins, millions of bacteria feed on nitrogen as they work. By adding it to your soil at this stage, you can temporarily rob your soil of nitrogen. However, if you allow your compost to fully decompose before you use it, you give the micro-organisms within it the chance to begin producing nitrogen and many other valuable nutrients, which you can then add to your soil.

Overleaf The soil prepared before planting as a mini potager area.

A species of bacteria known as Azobacter are the ones at work here – they are able to take atmospheric nitrogen, which plants cannot access, and release it into the compost to nourish your plants. Homemade compost may not always be as high in nitrogen as commercially produced composts, but if it is well made and properly matured, you can be sure it will not take nitrogen from your soil.

In my garden at Clondeglass I operate several compost heaps. While one is rotting down another is in the progress of being made. Because they are large, I get help when it comes to turning them.

Green material being added to a compost heap.

Making your own compost

So how do you make great compost? First, provide an area for making the compost. Make sure it is not in the way of anything important and that it has easy access for a wheelbarrow or two. You need several easily sourced things – air, nitrogen, lime (optional, see below), water, heat and bacteria. Only use items that are organic, exclude diseased material and avoid using cooked scraps from your kitchen, as these may attract rodents. When you start your first compost heap, you will be surprised by the amount of material that can be turned into valuable compost. Do not put in a pile of grass cuttings. Grass can be used, but it needs to be put in in layers, otherwise it will end up as a slimy mess. Remember that air is vital to assist in the process, so it helps to put in a layer of straw, small twigs or shredded newspapers, which are less dense.

The addition of a little lime will help to keep the compost 'sweet', as it will neutralise the acidity. Caution here. If your soil is alkaline, you may like to omit the lime from the mix. The reason for adding lime is that it will speed up the process of decomposition and you will have your homemade compost faster. To test your soil pH you will need to buy a kit from your local garden centre (see page 158). This will help you work out very quickly whether your soil is acidic, neutral or alkaline. Remember that in large gardens the pH can vary from one area of the garden to another, so it's a good idea to do several tests and label them as you go so they don't get mixed up. If you do use lime, ground lime is probably best. There are other limes available, but be careful as many of these can be caustic and will damage plants and roots. Only use a very small amount of ground lime, sprinkled lightly over layers approximately

30cm (12in) deep. This lime can remain active over many years, so if you have any doubts always seek the advice of an expert or ask at your local garden centre.

By turning your compost heap at least once in the rotting process you help to prevent compaction and add much-needed air. This also encourages faster decomposition. At this point I should mention heat. As your compost heap develops and grows, the temperature starts to rise. This is a normal part of the rotting process. In winter, when the weather is cold, it's much more difficult to maintain the necessary heat. A good trick is to cover the top with an old carpet. This will allow air in but help prevent heat escaping.

Nitrogen can also be added, and one of the best sources is animal manure – cow, horse or chicken. Manure can be very rich, though, so dividing it between layers is always a good idea. I also add a sprinkling of calcified seaweed, an excellent organic fertiliser. Other organic fertilisers that can be sprinkled in for extra nitrogen include dried blood and bone meal. Do not over-use these, though. I recommend a light dusting from time to time while you are creating the compost heap.

There are all kinds of compost heaps and some of the best are ones you construct yourself. They can be made of timber and I've seen superb ones made of decking boards with strong posts. If creating one yourself, remember that you will need to have access to the front. Having a slatted front it will make it easier as you build a heap. Timber posts with wire can also be used, and bricks with timber slats for the front are good too. Plastic barrels that have not had chemicals stored in them are sometimes available, but these need

to have holes drilled in the sides. There are also many commercial types available, most of which are plastic. These are usually more suited to the smaller garden. Choosing which heap you buy or construct all depends on the quantity of compost you need.

All of this sounds like a lot of hard work, but making your own compost is usually spread over many weeks and months, which makes the job a lot easier. The benefits are fantastic and, as I said at the beginning, your compost is worth its weight in gold.

A simple timber latted compost heap.

Protecting your Plants

The walls surrounding Clondeglass protect it from animals such as deer and rabbits, and also help to keep foxes and badgers at bay. They provide some shelter from the elements but, as in all gardens, protecting the plants is essential. This protection takes many different forms. Hedges, glasshouses, cloches, frames and a polytunnel all play their part.

A view of the polytunnel with spring tulips and narcissi in the foreground, which also shows the newly planted yew hedge.

Hedges

At Clondeglass, I have to consider the damage that wind can cause. While laying out the design, I included several native hedges within the walls, running across the garden both a quarter and three-quarters of the way up. These were put in for several reasons: primarily to add extra protection from wind within the garden, but also to provide areas for nesting native birds and to encourage beneficial insects to visit the garden.

The native hedges are made up of at least a dozen different native plants that can be found growing in hedges all over Ireland, and were purchased as small rooted cuttings from Coillte, a company that deal commercially in forestry. Unfortunately, they no longer sell hedging plants, so I consider myself very lucky.

In addition, a yew hedge was planted the full length of the garden from north to south. This offers protection from winds that run across the garden and also acts as a perfect backdrop to the borders. Being evergreen, it works superbly to help divide the garden and create a sense of different areas.

Throughout the garden, five or six other hedging plants have been used, including roses such as 'Wild Edric'. Each has been carefully chosen and planted. They have all settled in and, apart from providing beauty and interest, they do a marvellous job at helping to protect the garden in winter, especially from wind. This protection has turned out to be vital for many plants growing inside the walls at Clondeglass, which would otherwise have been severely damaged by exposure to cold wind.

Cloches and greenhouses

Cloches are also used extensively around the garden, especially over the winter months and in early spring. They act as miniature greenhouses and are especially valuable as a way of stopping frost from burning new shoots. I find they also help to warm soil, allowing me to sow seeds early in spring. When growing young plants, I place miniature cloches made from clear plastic bottles over them, which help to protect them and encourage growth. Take a 2-litre clear mineral water bottle and cut it in half, leaving the lid on. This can then be removed for ventilation. These homemade cloches are wonderful in the polytunnel (see right), can also be used outside, and are especially valuable when starting seedlings.

I have an ambition to erect a Victorian-style greenhouse at the south end of the garden. This would help expand the range of plants I can grow, assist with propagation and help get plants growing early in the year.

Horticultural fleece

Horticultural fleece is an extremely effective way of protecting plants from early frosts, when the new shoots begin to grow and are at their most vulnerable. It needs to be secured carefully to prevent it from blowing away.

Mulch

Well-rotted homemade garden compost or well-rotted farmyard manure put on in a thick layer over or surrounding a plant helps to prevent frost from penetrating deeply into the ground, and also adds extra nutrients to the soil as it decomposes. As well as protecting and helping to keep the soil warm in the colder months, mulch is also very good at keeping moisture in the ground during dry periods.

Polytunnels

With the big surge of interest in growing your own vegetables, polytunnels have increased in popularity. Originally, my dream was to have a large lean-to glasshouse on the south-facing wall. However, finances were tight to start with, and so putting a polytunnel in place made sense. I have never looked back. It made a huge difference to growing, allowing me to have many different edible crops earlier than if I'd grown them in the open garden. I can grow year-round salad crops and some vegetables and flowering plants. I recommend you go for the largest you can accommodate (mine is approximately 17m/55ft long and 8.5m/28ft wide) and, obviously, consider that it may not be the most attractive feature to look at. However, it is one of the joys of my garden – a place I can retreat to on wet days, a place where I can grow all kinds of extra plants, bringing in everything from salads to strawberries ahead of the rest of the garden. The atmosphere in the polytunnel is very special, with all the wonderful fragrances that are captured within.

I chose a polytunnel where the sides could be easily raised to allow ventilation in summer. These roll up neatly and allow air to circulate, which is very important when growing edible crops. The next thing I did was to put in a path running through the centre of the tunnel. It's made of decking timber, which had been well treated with preservative in advance of installation. At the very end of the tunnel is a decking area – a very useful place to keep tender container plants in winter.

One of the most important things when laying out a polytunnel is to allow for water. I laid a pipe bringing water from my well to the tunnel. I also recommend a large water barrel. I always keep a watering can close by. I use a Haws watering can because of its ergonomic shape, which makes it easy to carry water from one end of the tunnel to the other.

When erecting a polytunnel, it is important to install electricity. This allows for an electric propagator and lighting and also, if needed in severe weather, an electric heater. It's vital when using electricity outdoors to have a professional electrician install the proper cables, especially when there's water around. This work can be done at the beginning and will add to the comfort and usefulness of the polytunnel.

Early on, a priority was the preparation of the soil. Knowing that I wanted the polytunnel to be very productive, I decided to incorporate plenty of organic matter into the soil. The ground was initially double dug, and this meant that stones could be removed and organic compost could be added.

I was anxious to use organic methods to eradicate slugs. I used Nemaslug, an organic and safe way to control slugs and snails and to prevent the soil from being contaminated with chemical slug killers.

Tomatoes

The first year I had my polytunnel I grew a huge range of tomatoes, experimenting and trying different types. The key reason was for flavour, and after trying about 15 different varieties, I returned to many of the old traditionals such as 'Gardener's Delight', as well as bite-sized tomatoes, a must in salads. Varieties I remember growing as a boy include 'Moneymaker', 'Ailsa Craig' and 'Alicante', all with flavours that make your mouth water as you bite into them.

My earliest memory of tomatoes is when I was about 10 or 11 years old. Each summer I used to visit my grandparents' garden. My grandfather had a small greenhouse that he filled with tomatoes each year. One summer, I recall going into the greenhouse and experiencing the fantastic rich smell of tomatoes. Some of them were ripe and, without permission, I picked one and ate it. The taste was superb – mouthwatering and full of flavour. I remember thinking that I would be in big trouble, though nothing was said. So my first experience of picking a home-grown tomato was good and this encouraged me in later years to try again.

A few years ago Tanguy de Toulgoët, a French gardener, assisted me with the garden at Clondeglass and was especially helpful after the period when I had been very ill. Tanguy is very fond of tomatoes and grew numerous varieties. These were grown in prepared soil within the polytunnel. The marvellous thing about tomatoes is that they're easy to grow from seed. If seed is not your thing you can buy small plants at most garden centres. If you have space, it's a good idea to try a few varieties, as it can help with the pollination. If, however, space is limited, a growbag can be useful and some are specially made for growing tomatoes. They can take four or five plants but, to get a good crop, I recommend that you keep to three. This will give plenty of room and allow the tomatoes to develop fully.

Tomatoes also grow well in large containers. Make sure the containers are clean and have good drainage. The dimension of the pot should be a minimum of 30cm (12in). Purchase the best-quality compost you can buy and, if starting the tomatoes off as small plants, gently water them. Tomatoes resent extremes and do not like to be over- or under-watered.

'Gardener's Delight'

'Ailsa Craig'

'Moneymaker'

Salads

The polytunnel helps to provide lettuce for salads and I grow many different types. Some of the most reliable varieties are:

– 'Lolla Rossa', an Italian loose-leaved lettuce with a lovely red tinge, which can transform the look of a salad. It has a very good flavour and can be grown inside or out.

– My mother's favourite, 'Little Gem'. This superb early compact lettuce is ideal for use in sandwiches. It has a delicious flavour and is easy to grow.

– 'Buttercrunch', a traditional compact lettuce forming a good heart. It has excellent flavour and is very slow to bolt.

I would normally plant these in succession, buying seeds and planting a few at a time.

Herbs

The polytunnel offers warmth and dry soil, allowing for a range of herbs to be planted. I went for traditional, easy herbs, putting in a row of thyme. In the warmth of summer, I also include a row of basil and in one corner I have a dwarf rosemary. The scent from these on a warm, sunny day fills the air in the tunnel and immediately gets my tastebuds working as I think of the wonderful dishes in which I can use them. There's no comparison between fresh and dried herbs. To have fresh herbs available as needed can make a great difference to the taste of a dish you're cooking. The polytunnel offers a Mediterranean climate, allowing these herbs to fully enjoy the warmth and shelter the polytunnel provides. Also taking advantage of these conditions, I planted a small hedge of lavender on each side of the path. I went for a very particular named variety called 'Richard Gray'. This lavender has extra silvery grey foliage and dark rich purple flowers. What drew me to this was the first time I picked and smelled the flower. To me, it was stronger than any other lavender I have grown. The scent is rich and powerful and adds wonderfully to the overall scent in the polytunnel when in full flower. The contrast between the dark purple flowers with the light silver foliage is stunning, and the flowers are perfect for drying.

Annually, I sprinkle seeds of calendula, the pot marigold, into some of the beds. This beautiful orange annual thrives in the polytunnel and the edible petals can be used in salads, adding an exotic splash of orange as well as a peppery flavour. They are simple and easy to grow, and usually self-seed. A little borage gives brilliant blue flowers, which are also edible and good for use in summer drinks. When relaxing with a Pimms on a summer's day, some floating blue borage flowers can transform and add a touch of magic to the drink. A very simple plant to grow from seed, I have also found that bees love the borage too, which is good for general pollination in the tunnel.

Flowers

I also use my polytunnel to provide cut flowers for the house. It gives me the opportunity to grow some roses that don't enjoy the wet climate. This started as an experiment and turned out to be very successful. This year, I have added more varieties. The first to go in were two plants of the rose 'Harry Edland', one on each side of the door. This beautiful mauve rose is one

Salad leaves.

of the strongest scented roses I grow. The fragrance is delicious, rich and sweet, and conjures up the essence of summer. Other roses I've tried this year include 'Louis XIV', a sumptuous rose with a rich, deep-red flower. 'Empereur de Maroc' is also a dark red with a superb, rich scent. These roses are never happy outside, as they don't enjoy the rain. The polytunnel offers the chance for them to develop flowers and fill the air with scent. Behind the roses, I put in a row of regal lilies (*Lilium regale*), to use as a cut flower. When in full flower, you want to linger to enjoy the rich fragrance that fills the air.

On the other side of the polytunnel, I grow some chrysanthemums, to provide late cut flowers. These include 'Emperor of China', a very beautiful pale pink with a dark centre. They grow 90–120cm (3-4ft) high and I usually use bamboo canes to stake them. They are wonderful for cutting and flower late, usually from October onwards, providing much-needed colour at that time of year. The exquisite quilled petals set it apart from others, giving it a lighter, more elegant look.

The polytunnel allows me to grow some tender, special plants, and the first to be planted into the ground was a compact form of *Erythrina crista-galli*, commonly called the cockspur coral tree. I had grown this exotic plant many years ago and had lost it. I was reintroduced to it on my travels around Italian gardens, where I saw plants in full flower. The brilliant red pea-shaped panicles of flowers are instantly eye-catching. In full flower it is a feast of scarlet red, lobster-claw-like blooms. The plant is the national flower of Argentina and Uruguay. In the northern hemisphere it flowers between April and October and loses all its foliage in winter.

This autumn and winter, I used the polytunnel to bring in a small collection of *Brugmansia*, commonly known as angel's trumpets. I had planted these fabulous, exotic trumpet-flowered plants in containers and placed them in the garden to provide a summer display. Not being frost-hardy, I took them into the polytunnel where I covered them in fleece and kept them on the dry side. Unfortunately, the fleece did not allow enough air circulation – fungus hit and the plants had to be cut back. They are regrowing and the polytunnel played an important role in protecting them. I also did this with a variegated *Tibouchina*, a beautiful exotic with several colours in its foliage and bright ultraviolet single flowers. The flowers seem to glow and give a sense of far away places.

The polytunnel provides the perfect shelter for my collection of agaves. Agaves are those plants that you always see when you travel around the Mediterranean: large, bold, spiky foliage in giant rosettes. I like the variegated varieties, which need a little more protection in winter, though don't mind being allowed to dry out. Again, they are used in containers as accent plants in sunny, warm spots to add an exotic touch to the garden. I'm always conscious that they can be dangerous, especially with children around, because the spikes on the leaves are sharp. A trick I learned many years ago was to use a wine cork on top of the spikes as protection in areas where people got close.

Left Chrysanthemum 'Emperor of China'

Overleaf The inside of the polytunnel showing the well-prepared soil, decking timber path and the fact that the sides can be raised for ventilation. To the left are sunflowers, then tomatoes. On the right are sweetpeas.

Rhubarb and Rhubarb Forcers

Right Rhubarb developing. As a rough guide, it's ready to pull when the stem is the length of your wrist to your elbow.

Rhubarb

My grandmother was fond of rhubarb, and at the end of her garden was a large area devoted to growing it. When I was very young I can remember her teaching me how to pull rhubarb stalks correctly. Using both hands, you take a firm grip low down on the stalk, and gently but firmly wiggle it to help loosen it, then tug strongly to separate it from the crown. At the end of the pulled stem, you would have a thick, light-coloured piece. She would never cut the stalk, as the piece left behind would rot down and could cause problems to the crown. Her rhubarb patch had around 50 large clumps that were regularly used in spring and early summer. She was a wonderful cook and made rhubarb tarts. Her speciality was rhubarb and ginger jam. My task would be cleaning the stems and then chopping them into small pieces.

There are now many different varieties of rhubarb growing at Clondeglass. These include varieties such as 'Timperley Early', an old favourite that was used for forcing and is noted for its excellent flavour. One of my favourites is 'Canadian Red'. This is a bright red-stemmed variety. Each stem is slender and crimson in colour. Superb for cooking and of first class quality, it provides very tender stems. Then there is 'Victoria', and I'm sure this is the variety my grandmother grew. The stalks are red and green and have great flavour. Recently, Brian O'Donnell gave me a green variety from Donegal, which he recalled from his own childhood. As it has no name, I call it 'O'Donnell's Green'. This one makes very chunky jam and is much less inclined to dissolve, with the pieces staying more intact during and after cooking.

MRS HALL'S RHUBARB & GINGER JAM

4kg (8lb 10oz) rhubarb

4kg (8lb 10oz) sugar

50g (1¾oz) ground ginger

1 Wipe the rhubarb sticks with a damp cloth to clean them. Cut off the leaf parts and bottom stumps.

2 Cut into 2cm (0.25in) lengths with a sharp knife. Weigh and place in a large, heavy saucepan or preserving pot. Add the sugar and ginger. Leave to sit overnight to allow the sugar to dissolve.

3 Bring the mixture to the boil and simmer until a dark brown colour is achieved, stirring occasionally and being careful not to burn it on the bottom. This will take about 2 hours. The objective is to boil off the water content and to then caramelise the sugar and fruit into jam.

4 Test to see if the jam is set by placing a small amount on a cold saucer and letting it cool slightly. If the mixture wrinkles when moved with a finger, it is ready.

5 Take off the heat, allow to sit for a minute and skim off the scum of bubbles that forms on top. Ladle into sterilised jars and secure with a tight lid. Label and store in a cool dry place until needed.

Rhubarb is hardy and prefers cool weather. It is planted as crowns. These are made up of a central fleshy root system and large buds that are apparent in winter when the plant is dormant. Rhubarb is a greedy plant and it needs plenty of organic matter, such as well-rotted manure, to be added to the planting hole. This can be dug in underneath and around the crown but it's best to avoid placing it on top of the buds.

Plant the crowns 40cm (1ft 3in) apart and, if you have the space, place in rows 1m (3ft) apart. It pays to prepare the soil in advance by digging a large hole in a sunny, well-drained part of the garden. Ideally, the crowns should be lifted and divided every five or six years at the end of November. My grandmother did this, using an old bread knife, cutting large crowns into several smaller plants ready for replanting and discarding the old centre. Leave newly planted crowns alone for the first year without pulling any stems.

Rhubarb forcers

These used to be fairly common, but now are usually seen only in old gardens. Occasionally, an original rhubarb forcer will appear at auction but this is now rare. At Clondeglass, there are several that were made by hand at Kiltrea Bridge Pottery, Co. Wexford.

Place the forcer over the crown early in the year, putting the top in place, and surround it with fresh rotting manure. The rotting manure generates heat and within a few weeks new leaf stalks will begin to rise inside the forcer. Because of the darkness within, these pink stalks will reach the full length to the top and at this stage they can be harvested, providing delicious, tasty, tender, pale-coloured stems – perfect for an early treat.

When harvesting is over – which can last several weeks – move the forcers to one side and incorporate any rotted manure into the surrounding soil. The crowns will now need a rest and it's a good idea to avoid harvesting from them again for at least 12 months so they can regain their strength. This is another reason to plant several crowns in your garden and use three or four forcers each year, as done at Clondeglass.

ORGANIC RHUBARB GREENFLY KILLER RECIPE

Rhubarb leaves are poisonous but can be put to good use. Shred 1.5kg (3lb 5oz) of rhubarb leaves, making sure you wear gloves. Place in a large saucepan and add 3.5 litres (6 pints) of water. Boil for 30 minutes. When the mixture is cool, put it through a strainer. (The strainer should be kept especially for this job.) To this solution, add 125g (4½ oz) soap flakes for every 2.5 litres (4 pints) and heat until dissolved, stirring occasionally (DO NOT use a wooden spoon – a metal implement is best.) Let this mixture cool, then pour into bottles. The bottles should be clearly marked with the word 'poison' and kept well out of the reach of children. This makes an effective, organic greenfly killer and, for best effect, it should be used within a few days of making it. If you've made too much and need to discard the surplus, take great care when doing so.

Resources

Nurseries and gardening suppliers

Barnhaven Primroses
World-renowned primrose specialists.
Plestin Les Grèves, France.
barnhaven.com

Cotswold Garden Flowers
Worcestershire, UK.
cgf.net - 01386422829

Fernhill Garden Centre
Co. Westmeath.
fernhillplantsplus.ie - 0906475574

Gee-up Horse Manure
Co. Cork, Ireland.
geeup.ie - 0214381485

Halls of Heddon
Dahlia and chrysanthemum specialists.
Northumberland, UK.
hallsofheddon.co.uk - 01661852445

Hayloft Plants
Suppliers of the oriental poppies
discussed in this book.
Worcestershire, UK.
hayloft-plants.co.uk - 01386562999

Microbe Solutions
Suppliers of EM (Effective Micro-
organisms). Co. Cork, Ireland.
microbesolutionsireland.com
0214552429

Mr Middleton Garden Shop
Plants, seeds, equipment and
treatments. Dublin, Ireland.
mrmiddleton.com

Nemaslug
Organic slug pellets.
nemaslug.co.uk - Also available from
Mr Middleton Garden Shop (above)

Neutrog Fertilisers
Suppliers of Seamungus and
Sudden Impact.
neutrog.ie - neutrog.com.au

Pan-Global Plants
Gloucestershire, UK.
Panglobalplants.com - 01452741641

West Country Nursery
Renowned lupin specialists.
Glourcestershire, Devon.
westcountrylupins.co.uk

Equipment and accessories

Farrow & Ball
Paint suppliers, Dorset, UK.
farrow-ball.com - 01202 876141

Haws Watering Cans
West Midlands, UK.
haws.co.uk - also available at gardenware.
com.au

Husqvana
Suppliers of outdoor machinery, including
the rotovator used at Clondeglass.
husqvana.com

Kiltrea Pottery
Suppliers of pottery, including the
terracotta urns and rhubarb forcers at
Clondeglass. Co. Wexford, Ireland.
kiltreapottery.com - 0539235107

Inspiration

Altamont Garden
Co. Carlow, Ireland.
Altamontgarden.com - 0599159444

Beth Chatto's Garden
Essex, UK.
bethchatto.co.uk - 01206822007

Chelsea Flower Show

Chelsea Physic Garden
London, UK.
chelseaphysicgarden.co.uk
02073525646

London, UK.
rhs.org.uk

Exbury
Hampshire, UK.
Exbury.co.uk - 02380891203

Glenveagh Castle
Co. Donegal, Ireland.
glenveaghnationalpark.ie

Johnstown Castle Walled Garden
Co. Wexford, Ireland
irishagrimuseum.ie - 0539184671

June Blake's Garden
Co. Wicklow, Ireland.
juneblake.ie - 0872770399

Kilmacurragh Garden
Co.Wicklow, Ireland.
botanicgardens.ie

Other information

Dermot's Secret Garden is broadcast
by RTÉ - www.rte.ie
RHS Plantfinder is published by
Dorling Kindersley - apps.rhs.org.uk/
plantfinder

Page numbers in *italics* refer to illustrations

A

Acacia baileyana 'Purpurea' 138–9, *138*

Acer palmatum dissectum 139, *139*

Aconitum 112

Agapanthus 24, 150

Agave 171

Allium *10–11*, *24*, *32–3*, 84, 150

    A. hollandicum 'Purple Sensation' 35

Altamont, Tullow 115

angel trumpets 171

Angelica 137

    A. sylvestris 'Vicar's Mead' 102, 137

aphids, lupin 84

Aquilegia 91

Aralia elata 21

    A. e. 'Argenteovariegata' *143*

    A. e. 'Aureovariegata' 142, *142*

    A. e. 'Variegata' 142

Ashwood Nurseries 124

Astrantia 82

Austin, David 86, 91

autumn 110–27

Award of Garden Merit (AGM) 142

Azara

    A. macrophylla 'Variegata' 142, 144

    A. serrata 'Aureovariegata' 144

Azotobacter 162

B

banana plant *24*, *30*, 31

basil 169

Beech Park, Clonsilla 115–6, 117

Begonia 'Bonfire' *38*

Bellefield, Co Offaly 115

Beta vulgaris 'Bull's Blood' 150

blackberry, wild 145

Blake, June 98

blood and bone meal 163

Blooms Nursery 102

borage 169

borders

    creating 16–38

    dividing areas 34–7

    East border 20–3, *45*

    Long border 28

    points of interest 38–9

    West border 24–33, 35, *54–5*

        box *4–5*

Brachyglottis repanda 'Purpurea' 132, *132*

Brown, Bob 64, 66

Brugmansia 171

Buddleja davidii 'Black Knight' *18–19*

    B. d. 'Nanho Blue' *30*

Butea 21, 25, *28–9*, 31

C

Calendula 169

Camassia 84

Canna 'Durban' *18–19*, *38*, 150, *150*

Cercis canadensis 'Forest Pansy' 137, *137*

Chatham Island Forget-me-not 62–3

Chelsea Flower Show 84, 132

Chinese tree peonies 69

Chrysanthemum 171

    C. 'Emperor of China' 171, *171*

Clarke, Jim 79

Clematis viticella 'Mary Rose' 35

cloches 166

cockspur coral tree 171

Coillte 166

cold, protecting against 69, 71, 166

colour 19, 40–127

    autumn and winter 110–27

    spring 42–79

    summer 80–109

compost 159, 162–3

Conan, John 132

Convallaria majalis 'Green Tapestry' *144*, 145

    C. m. var. *rosea* 145

    C. m. 'Variegata' 144–5

cordial, elderflower 135

Cordyline 30

Cosmos 96

Cotinus coggygria 'Grace' 47

Cotswold Garden Flowers 64

cottage at Clondeglass 8, 9, 14–15

Crocosmia 102–9

    C. × *crocosmiiflora* 'His Majesty' 102

    C. × *c.* 'Mount Usher' 150

    C. × *c.* 'Nimbus' 107

    C. × *c.* 'Prometheus' 107

    C. × *c.* 'Solfatare' *18–19*, 28, 102, *105*

    C. × *c.* 'Star of the East' 107

    C. 'Emily McKenzie' 107

    C. 'Firebird' 102, *102*, 107

    C. 'George Davison' *104*

    C. 'Lucifer' *10–11*, *24*, 28, 102, *103*, *107*, 137

    C. 'Rowallane' 35

Crocus 112

    C. sativus 102

Cross, Brian 132

crown imperials 43, 44–9, 150

Crûg Farm Plants *128*

Cushnie, John 78

D

Dacus, Carl 132

daffodils *6*, *34*, *42–3*, 101, 126–7

Dahlia 31, *32–3*, 98–101

    D. 'Arabian Night' 98

    D. 'Bargaly Blush' 150

    D. 'Bishop of Llandaff' 31, 95, 98

    D. campanulata 100–101

    D. 'Hillcrest Royal' 98, 150

    D. merckii 101

    D. 'Moor Palace' 98

    D. tenuicaulis 100

Daphne bholua 'Peter Smithers' 35

Darts, Francesca 66

Dicentra 56

Dierama 'Guinevere' *28–9*

Digitalis purpurea 'Pam's Choice' 91

Dillon, Helen 69, 102

diseases, mildew 90

Dobbin, Peter 13

drainage 13, 158

Duff, Gavin 14

Duignan, Carmel 79, 132, 138–9, 145

E

Ealeagnus pungens 'Quicksilver' *32–3*

earwigs 100

East Border 20–3, *45*

edging 21

elderflower cordial 135

electricity, installing in a garden 167

EM (Effective Micro-organisms) 72, 117, 158–9

Erythrina crista-galli 171

Eupatorium *18–9*, 31

Euphorbia *32–3*

    E. characias 48–9

Exbury Gardens, Exbury 118

F

Fan Fi Pan 79

Fernhill Gardens, Dublin 132

fertilisers 117, 163

    seaweed 63

Ficus 'Digitata' 38

figs 38

Findlater, Miss Doris 118

fleece, horticultural 166

flowers, cut 169–71

foliage 128–53

    golden-leaved plants 148–53

    purple-leaved plants 130–9

    variegated plants 140–7

foliar feeds 101

forcers, rhubarb 177

forget-me-nots *58*, *61*

foxgloves 91

Fritillaria imperialis 43, 44–9, 150

    F. i. 'Argenteovariegata' 47, *47*

    F. i. 'Aureomarginata' 47, *47*

    F. i. 'Maxima Lutea' *46*, 47

    F. i. 'The Premier' 47

    F. i. 'Prolifera' 47

    F. i. 'Striped Beauty' 47

    F. i. 'William Rex' 47, *48–9*

frost 38, 71, 166

Fuchsia excorticata 'Purpurea' *130*, 132, *133*

G

Galanthus 114–7

G. 'Cicely Hall' 116
G. *elwesii* 115
G. *elwesii* 'Barnhill' 117
G. 'Emerald Isle' 116
G. 'Flore Pleno' *117*
G. 'Hill Poe' 116, *116*
G. 'Irish Green' 116
G. 'Kildare' 116, *117*
G. 'Kilkenny Giant' 116
G. 'Lady Ainsworth' 116
G. 'Lady Moore' 116
G. *nivalis 114*, 117
G. n.f. *pleniforus* 'Lady
    Elphinstone' 115
G. 'The O'Mahony' 116
G. *plicatus* 'Wendy's Gold' 115,
    116
G. 'Robin Hall' 116
G. 'Rowallane' 116
G. 'Straffan' 116–17
Gallagher, Eimear 117
Gaoithín, Séan Ó 63
Gee-up 159
Geranium 35, 91
    G. *psilostemon* 35
    G. 'Rozanne' 35, 91, 98
Giant Snowdrop Company 116
Glenveagh Castle, Donegal 29, 63
golden-leaved plants 148–53
    Philadelphus coronarius 'Aureus'
        151
    Rhus typhina 150
    Ribes sanguinem 'Brocklebankii'
        151
Goliath Group 95
grass *4–5*
grass cuttings 162
Great Dixter, Northiam 57, 98
greenfly 84, 177
greenhouses 166
Gypsophila 96
    G. 'Bristol Fairy' 96
    G. 'Flamingo' 96

H

Hamamelis 112–13
    H. × intermedia 'Jelena' 112, *112*
    H. mollis 112, *113*

Hayloft Plants 95
hedges and hedging 166
    box *4–5*
    yew 25, 35, 72, 166
Helleborus 124–5
    H. orientalis 124
    H. 'Pink Spotted Lady' *124*
    H. 'Pretty Ellen Red' *124*
    H. 'White Spotted Lady' *124*
Herbert, Reverend William 118
herbs 169
Higa, Dr Teruo 159
horse manure 159, 163
horticultural fleece 166
hostas 107
Hyacinthus 34, *45*, 50–3
    H. 'Anna Marie' 52, *53*
    H. 'Ben Nevis' 50, 52, *53*
    H. 'Blue Peter' 52
    H. 'Chestnut Flower' 52, *53*
    H. 'City of Haarlem' 52
    H. 'Delft Blue' 52
    H. 'Gipsy Princess' *51*, 52
    H. 'King of Great Britain' 51
    H. 'Lady Derby' 52
    H. 'Menelik' 52, *53*
    H. 'Midnight Mystique' 52
    H. 'Orange Boven' *50, 51*
    H. 'Orange Queen' 52
    H. 'Pink Royal' *51*
    H. 'Queen of the Blues' 52
    H. 'Woodstock' 45, 50, *51*, 52
Hydrangea 158

I

An Irish Florilegium: Vol II 118

J

jam, Mrs Hall's rhubarb and ginger
    174
Japanese maples 139
Japanese tree peonies 35, 69
jars 38
Joe Pye weed *18–19*, 31
Johnson, Barney 142
Johnstown Castle, Powerscourt 21
Jupe, Angela 115, 116

K

Kennedy, Joe 64
Kenny, David *86*
Kilmacurragh 63
Kiltrea Bridge Pottery *26–7*, 38,
    177

L

Laburnum 135
    L. vossii 134
Lakemount, Glanmire 132
Land Commission 13
Laurus nobilis 4–5
Lavendula 'Richard Gray' 169
Lemoine 70
lettuce 169
Lilium 18–19, 28
    L. lancifolium 18–19
    L. regale 171
lime 158, 162–3
Liriodendron tulipifera
    'Aureomarginatum' 145, *145*
Lloyd, Christopher 57, 98
Lobelia tupa 101
Lomandra confertifolia Ssp.
    rubiginosa 38
Long border 28
lupin aphid 84
Lupinus 82–5
    L. 'Beefeater' 84
    L. 'Desert Sunset' 84
    L. 'Gladiator' 84
    L. 'Manhattan Lights' *82*, 84
    L. 'Masterpiece' *82*, 84
    L. 'Persian Slipper' *83*
    L. 'Polar Princess' 84
    L. 'Red Arrow' *82*
    L. 'Red Rum' 84
    L. 'Saffron' *84–5*
    L. 'Tequila Flame' *82*

M

McDonogh, Peter 82
Macer, Nick 79, 139
McIlwaine, Cherrie 82
Magnolia 25, 35, 43, 72–9
    M. 'Black Tulip' 25, *74–5*, 76

M. denudata 'Yellow River' 25, 78,
    78
M. grandiflora 79, 146
M. g. 'Clondeglass Gold' *146*
M. g. 'Saint Mary' 79
M. 'Iolanthe' 76
M. × kewensis 'Wada's Memory'
    79
M. × loebneri 'Leonard Messel'
    25, 72, *73*, 76
M. sapanensis 79
M. 'Star Wars' 25, 35, 76, *76*
M. stellata 'Jane Platt' *77*, 78
M. 'Vulcan' 76
M. × wieseneri 78, 79
manure 158, 159, 163, 166
maple, Japanese 139
Marlfield Garden Centre 142
Masterson, Larry 7
Microbe Solutions 158
mildew 90
Miller, Robert 116–17
Mr Middleton's Garden Shop 57
Mrs Hall's rhubarb and ginger jam
    174
Montbretia 102–109
Mount Usher Gardens, Wicklow 145
mulch 72, 166
Musa basjoo 30, 31
Muscari 78
Myosotidium hortensia 62–3
    M. h. 'Alba' 63

N

Narcissus 34, *45*, 50, 54–5, 126–7,
    127
    N. 'Brackenhurst' *42–3*
    N. 'Rijnveld Early Sensation' 127
    N. 'Rip Van Winkle' 127
National Botanic Gardens,
    Glasnevin 118
National Collection of Hyacinth
    Varieties 51, 52
Nelson, Charles 118
Nepeta 56
    N. 'Six Hills Giant' *3*, 35, *36–7*, 91
Nerine 118–23
    N. bowdenii 118

N. 'Dame Alice' *123*
N. 'Fleeting Dream' *123*
N. 'Glensavage Gem' 118
N. 'Natasha' *123*
N. *sarniensis* 118
N. *s.* 'Janet' *119*
N. 'Strawberry Parfait' *123*
N. 'Tweedledee' 118
N. 'Tweedledum' 118
Nicotiana 96
nitrogen 159, 163
Nolan, Anna 35, 76
Nymans 76

O

O'Brien, Seamus 63
O'Donnell, Brian 135, 174
Ophiopogon planiscapus 'Nigrescens'
    31
    O. p. 'Nigrescens Variegata' 146,
    147
oriental poppies 94–7

P

Paeonia 68–71
    P. 'Black Pirate' *71*
    P. 'Chromatella' 70–1, *70*
    P. 'Duchesse de Mornay' *68*, 69
    P. 'Qing Long Wo Mo Chi' 69
    P. *rockii* ('Rock Variety') 70
    P. *suffriticosa* 68, 69
    P. *s.* 'Dou Lu' 70
    P. *s.* 'Rimpo' 70
    P. 'Ying Luo Bao Zhu' 69
Pan-Global Plants 79, 139
pansies 58
Papaver orientale 94–7
    P. o. 'Beauty of Livermere' *95*
    P. o. 'Patty's Plum' 7, 95, *95*, 96
    P. o. 'Princess Victoria Louise' *94*,
    95
    P. o. 'Ruffled Patty' 95
Penstemon 96
peonies, tree 35, 68–71
pests
    earwigs 100
    greenfly 177

lupin aphid 84
slugs and snails 98, 167
whitefly 101
pH, soil 158, 162
Philadelphus coronarius 'Aureus'
    151, *151*
Pimm family 13
Polyanthus 'Amethyst Cowichan' *64*
    P. 'Blue Cowichan' *67*
    P. 'Francesca' 64, *65*, 66
    P. 'Red Indian' *67*
polytunnels 167–73
poppies, oriental 7, 94–7
Potentilla × *hopwoodiana* 10–11
pots 26–7, 38, *38*, *39*, 66
Primula 31, 43, *45*, 64–7
    P. 'Drumcliffe' 64, *67*
    P. 'Garryarde Guinevere' 64
    P. 'Harbour Lights' 66
    P. 'Inisfree' 64
    P. 'Irish Sparkler' 64
    P. 'Jack in the Green' *67*
    P. 'Julius Caesar' 64
    P. 'Kinlough Beauty' 64
    P. 'Red Indian' *67*
    P. 'Spice Shades' 66
    P. 'Tawny Port' 64
protecting your plants 164–77
pruning vines 138
purple-leaved plants 130–9
    Acacia baileyana 'Purpurea' 138–9
    Acer palmatum dissectum 139
    Brachyglottis repanda 'Purpurea'
    132
    Cercis canadensis 'Forest Pansy'
    137, *137*
    Fuchsia excorticata 'Purpurea' 132
    Sambucus 'Black Lace' 135
    Vitis vinifera 'Purpurea' 138
    Zanthoxylum piperitum 'Purple
    Leaved' 139

Q

Quearney, Thomas 57

R

Rheum palmatum 'Astrosanguiem'
    6, *136*

RHS Award of Garden Merit 102
RHS Plant Finder 44, 64, 117, 123
rhubarb 174–7
    'Canadian Red' 174
    Mrs Hall's rhubarb and ginger jam
    174
    'O'Donnell's Green' 174
    organic rhubarb greenfly killer
    recipe 177
    ornamental 6
    'Timperley Early' 174
    'Victoria' 174
rhubarb forcers 177
Rhus typhina 150
    R. *t.* 'Tiger Eyes' 28, *148–9*, 150
Ribes sanguinem 'Brocklebankii' 151,
    151
Rosa 21, 35, 38, 86–93, 166
    R. 'Bonica' 35, *89*, 91
    R. *canina* 110–11
    R. 'Dermot O'Neill' *86*
    R. 'Dortmund' *86*, *87*
    R. 'Empereur du Maroc' 90, 171
    R. 'Fragrant Cloud' 90
    R. 'Harry Edland' *86*, *88*, 169
    R. 'Irish Fire Flame' 90
    R. 'Louis XIV' 90, 171
    R. 'Pierre de Ronsard' *90*
    R. *rugosa* 86
    R. 'Shakespeare' *90*
    R. 'Veilchenblau' *92–3*
    R. 'Wild Edric' *86*, 90, 166
    R. 'William Shakespeare 2000' 91
    R. 'Zéphirine Drouhin' 91
rosemary 169
Rothschild, Nicholas de 118, 123
rotovators 157
Royal Horticultural Society 142
RTÉ 2, 7
Rubus fruticosus 145
    R. *f.* 'Variegatus' *140–1*

S

St. Anne's Park, Raheny 86
salads 169
Salvia patens 150
Sambucus 'Black Lace' *134*, 135, *135*
Sanguisorba menziesii 95

scale 19
Schefflera 21
    S. 'taiwaniana' *48–9*
Seamungus 158
seasons 19
seaweed 63, 163
Shackleton, David 115–6, 117
Sheeran, CJ 21
Shefflera macrophylla *128*
Shipp, Alan 51–2
Siberian wallflowers 150
Slieve Bloom Mountains, Co Laois 8
slugs 82, 98, 167
Smithers, Sir Peter 69–70, 118, 123
smoke bush, purple 47
snails 82, 98
snow 38
snowdrops 111, *112*, 114–7
soil 156–65
    drainage 158
    improving 158–9, 162–3, 167
    pH 158, 162
spring
    colour 42–79
squirrels, red *2*, 2
stock 91
Straffan House, Co. Kildare 117
Stuart, Graham 107
Sudden Impact 158
summer 80–109
sunshine, protection from 90

T

Taxus baccata 'Irish Yew' *36–7*
Thompson & Morgan 52
thyme 169
Tibouchina 171
tiger lily *18–19*, 28
tomatoes 168, *168*
topiary, yew 36–7, 38
Toulgoët, Tanguy de 7, 168
Trachycarpus 25
tree peonies 68–71
Tulipa *24*, 25, 31, 56–61, 111, 150
    T. 'Angélique' 35, *56*, 57, *57*
    T. 'Apricot Beauty' 57
    T. 'Carnaval de Nice' 60
    T. 'Dreamland' *42–3*

_T._ 'Estella Rijnveld' 60

_T._ 'Flaming Parrot' _60_

_T._ 'Flaming Spring Green' _60_

_T._ 'Huis Ten Bosch' _60_

_T._ 'Ile de France' 60

_T._ 'Innuendo' _61_

_T._ 'James Wild' 60

_T._ 'Pink Delight' 57

_T._ 'Pink Diamond' _4–5_

_T._ 'Queen of Night' _42–3_, 57, _60_

_T._ 'Queen of Sheba' _4–5_, 57

_T._ 'Uncle Tom' _58_

_T._ 'Westpoint' 57

Tulipomania 57

U

umbrella plant _48–9_

University of Washington
    Arboretum 79

V

variegated plants 140–7

    Aralia elata 'Variegata' 142

    Azara macrophylla 'Variegata'
        142, 144

    Convallaria majalis 'Variegata'
        144–5

    Liriodendron tulipifera
        'Aureomarginatum' 145

    Magnolia grandiflora 146

    Ophiopogon planiscapus
        'Nigrescens Variegata' 146

vegetables, polytunnels 167

Verbena

    V. bonariensis 28, _31_, _32–3_, 98,
        102

    V. rigida _10–11_, 31

Vico Morcote, Switzerland 118

vines 138

Vitis vinifera 'Purpurea' 138, _138_

Voorhelm, Peter 51

W

Wadda, Mr. K 79

Walker, Robert 132

wallflowers, Siberian 150

Walsh, Wendy 118

watering

    in polytunnels 167

    water supply 13

West border 14–33, 35, _54–5_

West Country Lupins 82, 84

West Country Nursery _84–5_

whitefly 101

wind 166

winter 110–27

witch hazel 112–13

Wynn-Jones, Bleddyn and Sue _128_

Wynne, Janet 64

Wynne, Miss Winifred 64

Y

yew 25

    hedging _34_, 35, 72, 166

    topiary _36–7_, 38

Z

Zantedeschia 'Mr Martin' _28–9_

Zanthoxylum piperitum 'Purple
    Leaved' 139

Acknowledgements

Peter and Maura O'Neill

Carmel Duignan

Bill O'Sullivan

Brian O'Donnell

Helen and Val Dillon

Rachel and Frank Doyle

Barry Doyle

Joan and James Bennett

Claire Boland

Tony Brady

Brendan Breen

Cathy Brooks

Julie Brown

Ray Brown

Susan Carrick and Gerry Harford

Jim Clarke

Finlay Colley

John Cooney

Brian and Rose Cross

Senator John Crown

Carl Dacus

Peter Dobbin

Gavin Duff

Fionnuala Fallon

Sheila Farrell

Claire Faulkner

Paul Gallagher

Natasha Hartey

Bob Haugh

Brian and Marie Hughes

Bill Kelly

Joe Kennedy

Sean Kennedy

David Kenny

Pat Kenny

David Kinsella

Carol Klein

Liz Leavey

Nick Macer

Larry and Hazel Masterson

Ray McArdle

Peter McDonald

Cherrie McIlwaine

John McNamara

Robert Miller

Pat Mitchell

Seamus Mitchell

Adelaide Monk

Derek Mooney

Seamus O'Brien

Sean O Gaoithin

Siobhan Phelan

Richard Power

Donald Pratt

Thomas Quearney

Michael and Johanna Roche

Brendan Sayers

Alan Shipp

Flip Schram

Mark Sheeran

Tanguy de Toulgoet

Tim Schram

Marrgarite Sheeran

Kathryn Smith

John Smyth

Rachel Towell

Glen Waldron

Louis Walsh

Patricia Weaver

Charlie Wilkins

Brian Wood